APPALACHIAN SAYINGS

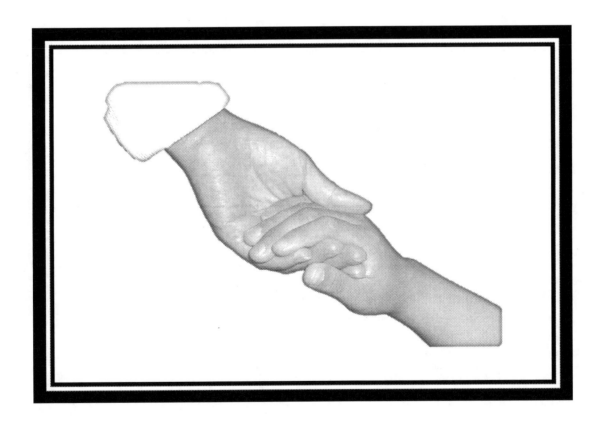

CHARLES AND SALLIE ANN HAYS

Order this book online at www.trafford.com
or email orders@trafford.com

Most Trafford titles are also available at major online book retailers.

Printed in the United States of America.

ISBN: 978-1-4669-9543-7 (sc)
ISBN: 978-1-4669-9544-4 (e)

Library of Congress Control Number: 2013908987

Trafford rev. 05/20/2013

 www.trafford.com

North America & international
toll-free: 1 888 232 4444 (USA & Canada)
phone: 250 383 6864 ♦ fax: 812 355 4082

CONTENTS

CHAPTER ONE Items 1-50 1
CHAPTER TWO Items 1-50 5
CHAPTER THREE Items 1-50 9
CHAPTER FOUR Items 1-50 12
CHAPTER FIVE Items 1-50 15
CHAPTER SIX Items 1-50 18
CHAPTER SEVEN Items 1-50 21
CHAPTER EIGHT Items 1-50 24
CHAPTER NINE Items 1-50 27
CHAPTER TEN Items 1-50 31
CHAPTER ELEVEN Items 1-50 34
CHAPTER TWELVE Items 1-50 37
CHAPTER THIRTEEN Items 1-50 40
CHAPTER FOURTEEN Items 1-50 43
CHAPTER FIFTEEN Items 1-50 46
CHAPTER SIXTEEN Items 1-50 49
CHAPTER SEVENTEEN Items 1-50 53
CHAPTER EIGHTEEN Items 1-50 56
CHAPTER NINETEEN Items 1-50 60
CHAPTER TWENTY Items 1-50 63
CHAPTER TWENTY-ONE Items 1-50 67
CHAPTER TWENTY-TWO Items 1-50 70
CHAPTER TWENTY-THREE Items 1-50 73
CHAPTER TWENTY-FOUR Items 1-50 77
CHAPTER TWENTY-FIVE Items 1-50 81
CHAPTER TWENTY-SIX Items 1-50 85
CHAPTER TWENTY-SEVEN Items 1-50 89
CHAPTER TWENTY-EIGHT Items 1-50 93
CHAPTER TWENTY-NINE Items 1-50 97
CHAPTER THIRTY Items 1-50 100
CHAPTER THIRTY-ONE Items 1-50 104
CHAPTER THIRTY-TWO Items 1-50 107
CHAPTER THIRTY-THREE Items 1-50 110

CHAPTER THIRTY-FOUR Items 1-50..113

CHAPTER THIRTY-FIVE Items 1-50 116

CHAPTER THIRTY-SIX Items 1-50...119

CHAPTER THIRTY-SEVEN Items 1-50 123

CHAPTER THIRTY-EIGHT Items 1-50.. 127

CHAPTER THIRTY-NINE Items 1-50...131

CHAPTER FORTY Items 1-50... 135

CHAPTER FORTY-ONE Items 1-50.. 139

CHAPTER FORTY-TWO Items 1-50.. 143

CHAPTER FORTY-THREE Items 1-50.. 147

CHAPTER FORTY-FOUR Items 1-50.. 150

CHAPTER FORTY-FIVE Items 1-50.. 154

CHAPTER FORTY-SIX Items 1-50.. 158

CHAPTER FORTY-SEVEN Items 1-50 162

CHAPTER FORTY-EIGHT Items 1-50... 166

CHAPTER FORTY-NINE Items 1-50... 170

CHAPTER FIFTY Items 1-50... 174

CHAPTER FIFTY-ONE Items 1-50 178

CHAPTER FIFTY-TWO Items 1-50 182

CHAPTER FIFTY-THREE Items 1-50 186

CHAPTER FIFTY-FOUR Items 1-50 190

CHAPTER FIFTY-FIVE Items 1-50 193

CHAPTER FIFTY-SIX Items 1-50 197

CHAPTER FIFTY-SEVEN Items 1-50 201

CHAPTER FIFTY-EIGHT Items 1-50 205

CHAPTER FIFTY-NINE Items 1-50... 209

CHAPTER SIXTY Items 1-50.. 213

CHAPTER SIXTY-ONE Items 1-50... 217

CHAPTER SIXTY-TWO Items 1-50... 221

CHAPTER SIXTY-THREE Items 1-50... 225

CHAPTER SIXTY-FOUR Items 1-50...228

CHAPTER SIXTY-FIVE Items 1-50 231

CHAPTER SIXTY-SIX Items 1-50 235

DEDICATION

The best mother that one might ever want was named Sallie Ann Hays (Hounshell). She was brought into this world, full of vim and vigor, very much alive and kicking, on 25JAN1910, one hundred and three years ago. She was quite determined to make her mark, with or without the help of anyone else.

Sallie Hays graduated from Lees College of Jackson, Kentucky at a time when young intelligent women were never expected to attend any institute of higher education. That was totally a man's world. She married an L&N railroader, Courtney Hays, who became an alcoholic after his first two children (twins) were the product of a split egg. Norma Lee Hays died at birth and Donald Lee Hays lived for nineteen long years as a total invalid with no visible senses or capabilities, physical or mental. Sallie took care of Donald on a 24-7 basis for as long as he lived.

Her college degree was in education and she made certain that I received nothing but the best of educations. I had two teachers, one from the Hazard City School 'System' and one from the Sallie Hays 'System'. As a result, I had two sets of homework to do every night, her's and their's. My first book that I was forced to read was Webster's Dictionary. The best book that I was ever assigned to read was "Kidnapped" by Robert Louis Stevenson. And, there were many more that followed that first reading. What mother of today's world would take the time to make her son become more intelligent?

When Sallie was a young girl of about six, she started collecting what she called 'old sayings'. And, she insisted that I should follow her pastime. It was my first hobby and, we both agreed that I would, one day, publish them for other people to enjoy. Unsurprisingly, this book is dedicated to my Mother. And, if she can hear me up there in Heaven, I would tell her the following. I do miss those many learning sessions around our fireplace hearth during the cold winters of Eastern Kentucky at my hometown called Hazard which was named in honor of Oliver Hazard Perry. It was he who said, "We have met the enemy and they are ours."

FOREWORD

In the early days of my development, I noticed that most of the children in my neighborhood were each being reared in a third person sort of way. Instead of saying "No" to their child, parents would speak a small sentence of a more thoughtful or considerate nature. The word 'no' doesn't mean very much to a small child who has committed a wrongdoing of some type. What says a great deal more is to say something that he can identify with better. For example, when George Washington cut down the cherry tree, he should not have been told, "No, don't do that." A better way of handling that is to say, instead, "George, it is bad luck to kill any living thing, especially since your Father loves cherries so much." In one swift motion, George was introduced to several key words of wisdom; namely, bad luck, killing, Father and cherries. In one small statement, a large guilt trip was firmly established by one simple activity that a sensitive child might never forget.

I don't know how one should classify books of this type but my best guess is something like historical or philosophic collections. In truth, it was about the way in which we lived way back when. These little one-liners represented our way of remedial life before modern math or the Principal's Office was ever introduced. Names, characters and events have been modified slightly to enhance the storyline and to protect the innocent people, places and occurrences. Any resemblance to actual persons (living or dead) and all associated events at specific locations are strictly coincidental and totally unintended. If there are any hurt feelings or bad feelings felt by any readers of this book, I prefer to think of them as being freak happenings caused by both probability and chance.

That being said for the legal reasons of our modern society, I bid you adieu and I hope that you will enjoy this book which my Mother and I took almost 100 years to compile. Our book probably represents the oldest compilation time for any other manuscript, ever!

Never do another man's wife. If she can't go the route with just one man, then the trip to see her isn't worth the risk.

CHAPTER ONE
ITEMS 1-50

1-1: A dropped fork means that a man is coming to call.

1-2: If you are homesick, eat onions.

1-3: Being the first-born child of a large family means a lot of hard work. But, that's better than being the last-born child of a large family, one who is apt to be very lonely after a long time has passed.

1-4: Dead soldiers aren't the only victims of a great war and this not about empty bottles. What about their relatives who must grieve their passing for many long years after their death in battle?

1-5: The best cure for problems caused by feuding, fussing and fighting is reading, writing and arithmetic taught to the tune of a history stick.

1-6: Homemade beats store bought.

1-7: One stitch in time saves nine stitches later on.

1-8: It is not easy to teach old dogs new tricks.

1-9: Only one thing beats good leftovers and that is fresh fixings.

1-10: A rich man's family is a boy for him and a girl for her.

1-11: Charity doesn't begin with the purse, it begins with a sharing heart.

1-12: Cleanliness is next to Godliness.

1-13: We are a race of people who have always been days-long and dollars-short.

1-14: The price of oil and gasoline needs to be paid by CEO's and their attorneys.

1-15: As the crime rate increases, the number of registered lawyers also increases.

1-16: Saint Peter allows no attorneys through the pearly gates.

1-17: If a child has asthma, cut a sourwood stick longer than the child is and, when he or she grows taller than that stick, the child will be cured of asthma.

1-18: When you are sweeping, never touch the broom to anyone that is still breathing or that person will experience bad luck.

1-19: If you want to know whom you are going to marry, go to the water well and do this . . . . Hold a mirror into the air, with the water behind your hair. Study the looking glass that's in your hand. And, you will see the image of your intended man in the deep water that lies below.

1-20: Two measures of wealth in yesteryear was toilet paper and fly swatters. Corn cobs and fly paper were left to the common man.

1-21: It is bad luck to bring a hoe inside of the house.

1-22: Never miss a friend's funeral. No matter how far the trip, that's the last thing that you can do together.

1-23: It is a sign of good luck if you can pick up a straight pin with the pointed end looking right at you.

1-24: If your nose itches, someone is coming to visit you.

1-25: When your ears get warm, someone is talking about you.

1-26: An itching foot means that you are going to walk on strange ground.

1-27: To dream of money means that a fire will soon exist.

1-28: To dream about fire means that a wedding is soon to occur.

1-29: It is bad luck if a black cat crosses your path in front of you.

1-30: It means good luck if a stray cat decides to stay at your house.

1-31: If the bottom of your foot itches, then you are headed for someplace where you are not welcome.

1-32: A wedding will occur if you dream about death.

1-33: If you are talking about somebody and that person happens to walk in, there's one of two things that you ought to do. Say, "Speak of the Devil" and he will make his presence known. Or, you could say, "Speak of the Angel" and you will hear their wings flapping about.

1-34: It brings good luck to find a four leaf clover.

1-35: Three times for any single thing means a charmed thing.

1-36: It causes bad luck to walk under an inclined ladder.

1-37: Stepping over a broom brings bad luck.

1-38: Never spin a chair around on one leg. That brings bad luck to the twister.

1-39: To cure a sore throat, wrap a black stocking around your neck.

1-40: Be nice to old ladies or they might bring on knocking sounds.

1-41: If you can peel an apple skin and keep it all in one piece, do this. Throw it over your left shoulder and, when it lands, it will form the initials of your soul mate.

1-42: Bald men don't lose hair. They just make room for more.

1-43: Place a strand of hair in a pond of still water and it will become a snake later on.

1-44: Never look into a mirror after dark since that will bring bad luck.

1-45: Walk backwards ten steps and take a good look at the ground. If you see a hair, it will be the same color that your future mate will have.

1-46: If your right hand itches, you are going to shake hands. If your left hand itches, you are going to handle money.

1-47: Never let a large critter into your cave on a rainy night. The rain will make you wet.

1-48: Paddle your own canoe.

1-49: Poor people with too little money come together strongly. Rich people who have too much money, grow apart weakly.

1-50: Never step on a crack because that will break your Mother's back.

Never talk bad about your neighbor. That's a pissing contest which you will lose as time passes.

CHAPTER TWO
ITEMS 1-50

2-1: If you use curse words, you will never raise good gourds.

2-2: If you are hairy around the arms and chest, you will have good luck with the raising of hogs.

2-3: Burnt bread makes the cook's face turn red.

2-4: A fellow that says very little will lie much less than the man who talks too much.

2-5: A real blessing for the poor is that they are not overly concerned about all the things that they do not have. Instead, they seem to care more about what they do have.

2-6: What is to be will be but, what should not be, might be.

2-7: What comes free seems to go faster than that which was paid for in full.

2-8: The best thing to be learned from gamblers is that win more often than not.

2-9: All ears gets more respect than all-mouths.

2-10: Too much work and too little play is the wrong path to wander.

2-11: An apple a day leaves the worms with less to eat.

2-12: An axe won't cut very much without a grinding wheel.

2-13: Never cut your finger nails on a Sunday. That will bring you bad luck.

2-14: A thin onion skin means that a mild winter will follow.

2-15: At the end of one's rope is socially acceptable unless the hangman is involved.

2-16: Little kids get to play while big kids have to work.

2-17: A back seat driver drives more than the wagon. He or she drives everyone else crazy.

2-18: Bad news spreads fast but, good news is better received.

2-19: The baseball game begins after the fat lady sings our National Anthem. It ends after we run out of baseballs.

2-20: Banana noses are worse than fish lips.

2-21: Beetles are bugs that bug other beetles.

2-22: Beggars are losers who never try to be choosers.

2-23: Being behind the 8-ball is tough but, being behind on the rent is worse.

2-24: The best patch is from the same cloth.

2-25: Beware of the door that has too many locks.

2-26: Some days are better if properly ignored.

2-27: Too many people don't like work because it involves taking orders from someone.

2-28: Food that is hardest to prepare will always taste best for the person that stays in the living room and patiently anticipates their chewing time.

2-29: Time awaits nothing and nobody.

2-30: Fat as a pig is big but, fatter pigs always exist.

2-31: Big fish devour smaller fish.

2-32: A bird in the hand is worth two in the bush.

2-33: Break a mirror and you will be facing seven years of bad luck.

2-34: Birds of the same feather will flock together.

2-35: Number 13 is not a lucky number.

2-36: A watched pot takes too long to boil.

2-37: Too much water passing beneath your bridge is bad. But, too little water passing under the same bridge is worse.

2-38: Bless your pea-picking heart.

2-39: A watchtower is always watched.

2-40: Being black from working with coal dust might be bad but, dealing with the black ace of spades can be worse.

2-41: The way to a man's heart is through his stomach.

2-42: Some people try real hard to earn disrespect.

2-43: Lighting three pipes from one kitchen match will cause bad luck.

2-44: Two people can make beautiful music together but, add another person, and it usually means noise.

2-45: Blockheads are typically squares.

2-46: Wear as many hats as you can.

2-47: Some gamblers won't play cards on Friday the 13th.

2-48: If you carry everything on your shoulders, you will become tired more quickly.

2-49: Don't put your foot in your mouth.

2-50: When a hen crows, it means bad luck.

Stealing is the wrong way to get stuff. The right way to get stuff is to earn it.

CHAPTER THREE
ITEMS 1-50

3-1: Toot your own horn.

3-2: Smart people see the clouds but smarter ones grab their umbrellas.

3-3: After one door closes, another door will open for you.

3-4: If you got a bone to pick, choose wisely.

3-5: When the chips are down, better times are coming.

3-6: Bookworms learn more.

3-7: The best profession of all is to have been a breadwinner.

3-8: Break the ice if you will but, avoid getting wet.

3-9: If poverty is at your door, make sure that love is inside the house.

3-10: A bridge over troubled waters gives us the means to move on.

3-11: White or pink elephants are unacceptable. Only gray elephants are acceptable.

3-12: A broken heart is best mended by a change in attitude.

3-13: A window on the world is available to each of us that try.

3-14: Don't burn the candle at both ends.

3-15: A girl that whistles in public will have bad luck.

3-16: In the 1800's a wife would soon become divorced if she suffered from flatulence in a public place.

3-17: You can eat cake or have cake but, you can't do both.

3-18: A woman who does everything well will always be well criticized.

3-19: It's all right to butter someone up but, don't use tar and feathers.

3-20: If you have the world on a string, avoid scissors.

3-21: Butterfingered people must concentrate more.

3-22: People who wear masks are hiding from themselves.

3-23: Mayflies should remain outdoors but, never in your mouth.

3-24: You are what you eat.

3-25: Cauliflower ears are preferred over hog jowls.

3-26: You can't be in two places at once so, stop trying.

3-27: Write no one's life story until after they are deceased.

3-28: Call no coal miner happy until after he has died.

3-29: You can't keep a good man down.

3-30: The cutest women seem to have more headaches at bedtime.

3-31: You can't see the forest because of the trees.

3-32: The ideal marriage is when they both have a headache at the same time.

3-33: Young shoulders are incapable of holding older heads.

3-34: It helps a young marriage to have a cast iron stomach.

3-35: A dream about muddy waters means that bad luck will soon arrive.

3-36: Coffins don't have side pockets.

3-37: Castles in the clouds are better than no castles at all.

3-38: Cat got your tongue?

3-39: A loose screw matters much.

3-40: The cat's already out of the bag after you say, "For your ears only."

3-41: You have to take the good with the bad.

3-42: Children should be seen but, not heard.

3-43: You hit the nail right on its head.

3-44: A chip off of the old block.

3-45: Fallen fruit from the same tree doesn't wander too far away.

3-46: You would forget your head if it wasn't screwed on so tightly.

3-47: There is very little rest for the wicked.

3-48: Chisel or be chiseled says the chiselers.

3-49: A tall tale usually begins with a big fib.

3-50: Once upon a time, tee shirts were called underwear. Now they are called outerwear.

Adultery is not reserved for adults only. That applies for all those who are past puberty.

CHAPTER FOUR
ITEMS 1-50

4-1: An eight foot mast will ward off evil or cause evil.

4-2: Climb your ladder to its highest rung.

4-3: That rings a bell.

4-4: Sadly, Christmas comes but once a year.

4-5: Kissing with mistletoe over your head will bring you good luck.

4-6: Absence makes your heart grow fonder.

4-7: That's a horse of a different color.

4-8: Climb every wall that blocks your path.

4-9: If your spoon plucks an almond from the pudding, it means good luck.

4-10: If you want to get rid of ants, spread grits upon the ground.

4-11: If you want better flowers, use coffee grounds for aeration of the soil.

4-12: I am on cloud number nine.

4-13: Once loved is better than no love at all.

4-14: That's how the cookie crumbles.

4-15: A small round pebble in your pocket will protect you from evil.

4-16: Arthritis can be treated with magnets.

4-17: Thunder will cause milk to spoil.

4-18: Cobwebs in the grass is a sign that rain will soon arrive.

4-19: Cover your mouth when you yawn so that the Devil's spirit won't enter your body.

4-20: Colorful language does not require curse words.

4-21: That's icing on the cake.

4-22: Always carry a round metal disc for good luck.

4-23: It is bad luck to talk about something before it is finished.

4-24: Do not wear yellow. It brings bad luck.

4-25: The rain is coming down in buckets.

4-26: It's raining cats and dogs.

4-27: There are better ways to kill a dog than by hanging them.

4-28: An itching thumb means that visitors are coming.

4-29: If you get married on the first day of April, the wife will dominate.

4-30: Don't drink milk when you eat fish.

4-31: Young people should never sleep in the same bed that older people use.

4-32: Never get out of bed on the wrong side.

4-33: Be a cool cat.

4-34: A dropped apron means bad luck.

4-35: Count sheep before sleep.

4-36: Never buy a saw that has blood stains on the cutting teeth.

4-37: For some people, a paper bag over the head would be an improvement.

4-38: April showers bring May flowers unless you live in Kenosha.

4-39: A cracked bell will never ring true.

4-40: If you spill salt, it's bad luck for you. However, the spell can be broken if you throw a few grains of salt over your left shoulder.

4-41: If a baby of less than twelve months is imaged in a mirror, that child will die an early death.

4-42: If two people wipe with the same towel at the same time, they will soon quarrel.

4-43: There is no fool like an old fool.

4-44: Never look into a mirror if you are using a light from a candle.

4-45: Passing wine at the table with your right hand brings good luck.

4-46: He didn't go quietly. He croaked himself to death.

4-47: There is more than one way to skin a cat.

4-48: A falling star means that a death has occurred.

4-49: Never use another man's crutch. That brings bad luck.

4-50: If a girl is kissed seven times in one day, she will marry within a year.

Never kill any living thing because it is wrong to do so.

CHAPTER FIVE
ITEMS 1-50

5-1: A pair of baby shoes will protect you from bad luck.

5-2: Wind from the North is of little worth.

5-3: Warts are caused by handling frogs.

5-4: Don't cry your eyes out. You will need them later.

5-5: Don't become a thorn in someone's side.

5-6: Unmarried men have poorer health than married men.

5-7: Dreaming about money too much may bring on poverty.

5-8: White is worn by the innocent.

5-9: Dead men tell no tales.

5-10: Know when to quit.

5-11: The worst kind of mail does not involve bills. 'Dear John letters' do a lot more harm.

5-12: Never bake a cake if you are menstruating.

5-13: A two dollar bill will bring you bad luck.

5-14: Time flies.

5-15: Always tighten your belt before dining.

5-16: Never be too tied up.

5-17: Wrap a live, fuzzy caterpillar in a cloth sack and wear that sack around your neck if you have the whooping cough.

5-18: It is bad luck to discard the egg shells before the meal is finished.

5-19: Eggs in the henhouse are cheaper than a dime a dozen.

5-20: Without a leg to stand on.

5-21: Sage tea will cure baldness.

5-22: Money in a new wallet or purse will bring good luck.

5-23: A plain gold wedding ring will cure sore eyes.

5-24: Hang a banana stalk inside of the house to get rid of lice.

5-25: Sleeping in moonlight will cause craziness.

5-26: Rub a sty on the eye three times with a gold wedding ring and that sty will go away.

5-27: Don't bite off more than you can chew.

5-28: Keep your ear to the ground to hear what is coming.

5-29: Don't let your tongue hang out.

5-30: Walls have ears.

5-31: Beads worn by babies will cause clean teeth or full stomachs.

5-32: Drinking moonshine whiskey will cause a straight razor to get dull.

5-33: Bed bugs and beans will cure a fever.

5-34: Wear gloves when you bait fish hooks or set mouse traps.

5-35: If you want to catch more fish, don't smoke cigarettes.

5-36 A wasp that flies inside of a house will bring bad luck.

5-37: A swarm of bees means that death will come for someone that you know.

5-38: Don't count your chickens before they hatch.

5-39: Too many cooks in the kitchen can spoil the broth.

5-40: A smart eagle never flies alone.

5-41: Don't be a wall flower.

5-42: Big feet are a sign of great intelligence.

5-43: If you move to a new house, leave your broom behind.

5-44: Water is fattening.

5-45: Just a drop in the bucket.

5-46: Two heads are better than one.

5-47: Never judge a book by its cover.

5-48: Feeling bad is like being under the weather.

5-49: A Robin's nest near your house means good luck.

5-50: Things turn out best for people who make the best out of the way that things turn out.

Respect your mom and dad. They spent an awful lot of money and time in bringing you up to what you are. As a result, you owe them big time.

CHAPTER SIX
ITEMS 1-50

6-1: It is bad luck for a girl to marry a man whose last name begins with the same letter as does her own surname.

6-2: If you wash your hair in water from a March snowfall, you will always be lucky in life.

6-3: Being up against a wall is like being in water that is too hot. You need to move on.

6-4: You need to get out more often.

6-5: Never let the grass grow beneath your feet.

6-6: Kill a swallow and expect bad luck.

6-7: Lovesickness can cause your nose to bleed.

6-8: It is bad luck to let anyone to walk between you and your companion while walking together.

6-9: Variety is the spice of life.

6-10: Don't look a gift horse in the mouth.

6-11: A child born during the summer will be a smart one.

6-12: Odd numbers are luckier than even numbers.

6-13: A one-armed customer means bad luck.

6-14: It brings bad luck to a person if you turn their picture upside down.

6-15: Never place all of your eggs into one basket.

6-16: Grab the bull by his horns and hang on tightly.

6-17: If a child bites his nails, that child will develop a problem with nails that are too short.

6-18: Burning a hole in a dress will lead to bad luck.

6-19: Don't place the cart before the horse.

6-20: Real men don't wear coats that have tails.

6-21: Sitting on an empty trunk will cause bad luck.

6-22: A classic car is one that we praise but, don't drive.

6-23: If the sky is falling, you have had better days.

6-24: An early bird catches more worms.

6-25: The sweetest grapes always hang at the highest level.

6-26: Never throw a monkey wrench into the machinery.

6-27: Never wash any blankets during a month that has no 'r' in its name.

6-28: The sound of the owl is an omen of bad luck.

6-29: When you are peeling onions, place a piece of raw potato in your mouth.

6-30: It is lucky to travel somewhere on a Tuesday.

6-31: Never throw out the baby with the bath water.

6-32: Don't sweep anything under the rug.

6-33: The sky is the limit.

6-34: Don't be down in the dumps.

6-35: Drinks are on the house.

6-36: She's looks like a mangy old hound dog if ever I saw one.

6-37: Blow on a seedy dandelion and count the remaining seeds. That's how many lovers you will know in your lifetime.

6-38: Peacock feathers on the lawn means that hard times are ahead.

6-39: A mouth sore on the tip of the tongue means that a lie was told.

6-40: A white spot under the finger nail means that you have been lying to someone dear.

6-41: Easy street is where you ought to live.

6-42: Go fly a kite.

6-43: Slow and steady will win most races.

6-44: Don't be a stuffed shirt.

6-45: That model of automobile is a lemon.

6-46: Most men don't make passes at women who are wearing glasses.

6-47: The whole idea of life is to leave something behind that made a difference.

6-48: He said that she melted in his arms but no one has ever done that.

6-49: Don't eat your heart out. If you do, you won't live very long.

6-50: Go bother someone else. I've had enough.

Be different, go to Church on Sunday morning, not enough people attend.

CHAPTER SEVEN
ITEMS 1-50

7-1: The trick is to always have something up your sleeve.

7-2: Be as stubborn as a mule.

7-3: Something is rotten in Denmark.

7-4: He had egg on his face.

7-5: Give him enough rope and he will hang himself.

7-6: Watch out for the booger man.

7-7: Three nutmegs hung around the neck will cure boils.

7-8: It is a sign of good fortune to find a black pearl in your oyster.

7-9: Stub your right toes and you will have good luck. Stub your left toes and you will have bad luck.

7-10: Clean teeth won't decay.

7-11: Eating the last bit of food from a serving plate will cause bad luck.

7-12: Eat pig jowls and black-eyed peas for good luck.

7-13: Eating pickled pig's feet means you still have money in the bank.

7-14: They that go too fast, stumble more.

7-15: They that go too fast, observe less.

7-16: Too often, the closest grapes will be the unripe ones.

7-17: A strong stomach and a stout heart will take you farther than most.

7-18: London fog is thick enough to cut with a knife.

7-19: London fog is where the criminals hide.

7-20: Never mind what you just said, just eighty-six it.

7-21: Eat the gingerbread man before he grows a coat.

7-22: Men who eat a lot of bread will have plenty of hair on their chest.

7-23: If you want to break the spell of any bad luck, say "Bread and Butter."

7-24: Finding a safety pin will bring good luck.

7-25: A loose hair pin means that someone is thinking of you.

7-26: Thunder with a cloudless sky is a sign of good luck.

7-27: If three people make up a bed together, one of the three will become ill.

7-28: Never serve thirteen people at a single meal. That brings bad luck.

7-29: Empty cans make the most noise.

7-30: You are getting on my bad side.

7-31: Why must I wear a cap on my knee?

7-32: If you have a lock of his hair, where is the key?

7-33: Where are your jewels to be found, at the crown of your head?

7-34: What can shoulder blades cut?

7-35: What spans the bridge of your nose?

7-36: Could the roof of your mouth be shingled?

7-37: Should the crook in your nose go to prison?

7-38: Have you ever hammered any nails on your toes?

7-39: Does the palm of your hand offer coconuts?

7-40: Do you have an ear-of-corn or a corn on your toe?

7-41: Do your eardrums play for all drummers?

7-42: Don't calf-lick this job.

7-43: Loose lips sink ships.

7-44: Heels should not support heels.

7-45: I hit my crazy-bone.

7-46: There are many grades of liars including lovers, lawyers, fishermen and politicians.

7-47: Eyeteeth can't see anything but, eyeteeth can cause much pain.

7-48: Don't be a clock watcher.

7-49: In today's economy, be early in and late out.

7-50: Never ask for a funeral leave for a third cousin. That's not your immediate family.

Never take the name of anyone in vain for it is wrong to do so. And besides, they didn't name themselves. One of their two parents gave them their moniker.

CHAPTER EIGHT
ITEMS 1-50

8-1: Always hold your chin high.

8-2: Behind thine eyes thy beauty lies.

8-3: You are getting under my epidermis.

8-4: He's got eyes in the back of his head.

8-5: That's finger-licking good.

8-6: Keep your foot in the door.

8-7: If need be, place it past the transom.

8-8: Speak softly but carry a big stick.

8-9: Say what you mean and do what you say.

8-10: I don't like to wear glasses because I don't care to be called 'four-eyed'.

8-11: Got a frog in your throat?

8-12: Stretch your legs in the seventh inning.

8-13: I got it straight from the horse's mouth.

8-14: Don't be stone-faced.

8-15: Don't stab people in the back.

8-16: Never poison someone's mind.

8-17: He's got a pot belly.

8-18: Is your thumb green?

8-19: My hands are tied.

8-20: Keep you head out of the clouds.

8-21: Did you hear it through the grapevine?

8-22: Even hedgerows have openings.

8-23: Keep your heart at home.

8-24: Hot pants and cold hearts seem to be inseparable.

8-25: I am in it and I'm up to my neck.

8-26: It's written all over your face.

8-27: Don't let it go in one ear and out the other.

8-28: Snow on the roof doesn't mean that there is no fire down below.

8-29: Keep your head above water.

8-30: Light my fire.

8-31: Like father, like son.

8-32: Look before you leap.

8-33: Don't lose your head.

8-34: Too many hands can cause too little work.

8-35: His heart has wings.

8-36: Music will serve the savage beast.

8-37: Never hit below the belt.

8-38: Don't straddle the pole.

8-39: A picture is worth a thousand words but, a solution to an engineering problem, is worth a thousand pictures.

8-40: Today, the motherboard of all errors, lies somewhere inside of our computers.

8-41: Don' pull my leg.

8-42: My final job will be pushing up the daisies.

8-43: Let's put our heads together.

8-44: Put your thinking cap on.

8-45: That's a feather in your cap.

8-46: Put your money where your mouth is.

8-47: He's as queer as a two dollar bill.

8-48: He's got rocks in his head.

8-49: Try to keep a roof over your head.

8-50: Never grow roots at one location.

Show mercy to all the persons that you come into contact with, even the poor, the hungry and the homeless.

CHAPTER NINE
ITEMS 1-50

9-1: It is all right to snore at night. Hard working men can't help themselves. Snoring is caused by fatigue and sore muscles.

9-2: His second job is sawing logs at night.

9-3: Be a self-made man.

9-4: That girl will steal your heart.

9-5: Don't shoot your mouth off.

9-6: Sit on it.

9-7: Sleep on it.

9-8: That's a shot in the arm.

9-9: Be as snug as a bug in a rug.

9-10: Carry a few bread crumbs in your pocket for good luck.

9-11: Company is coming if buttered bread falls on the floor with the buttered side down.

9-12: Always plant potatoes with their eyes pointed upward.

9-13: If bubbles float toward you, you will always have money.

9-14: Teeth that are spaced wide apart indicate happiness.

9-15: A gap between the two front teeth identifies a wanderer.

9-16: Leave the lid of a tea pot open and someone will visit you.

9-17: Don't sit on the dining table or you will soon get married.

9-18: Sweeping in the darkness will bring bad luck.

9-19: A bride's first kiss must be answered with tears.

9-20: Spilt salt brings on a quarrel.

9-21: A praying mantis is an agent of the devil.

9-22: If you want to catch more fish, pray to them first.

9-23: Truth is known to exist in certain parts of the USA but, not in Washington DC. There, the truth is rarely known.

9-24: In the early 1800's, the State of Washington tried to change its name because they didn't want to be identified with the corrupt District of Columbia.

9-25: Wrong words uttered at a bad time can light a flame that lasts too long.

9-26: It is never very wise to compliment someone just prior to asking them for a favor.

9-27: Ignore what you can but, enjoy what's left.

9-28: Our daily work allows us to survive but, our activities at night can threaten our very survival.

9-29: A good conscience is our tool to help us avoid most temptations.

9-30: Plagiarism is defined as stealing from another person's creativity.

9-31: If an independent writer pens something that is similar to another person's work, but not identical, then that is called art.

9-32: Climbing a mountain is the best way to admire a valley.

9-33: My favorite mountain now has an ugly highway on it and children don't climb the hill like they once did.

9-34: It is hard to do something right and good because it is easier to do something wrong and bad.

9-35: Doing things correctly gives us pleasure and the motivation to continue that practice.

9-36: Doing things wrongly affects our morals and our ability to understand cause and effect.

9-37: Too many of us pattern our behavior after television, movies and books. I got mine from my Methodist Church and my parents.

9-38: You can pray about the truth freely but, it is far more difficult to pray about lies.

9-39: Telling a white lie can be a finite thing but telling the truth leads us to infinity.

9-40: If homely lies are so unattractive, why are handsome truths so palatable?

9-41: If a person answers a question very quickly, he or she is probably telling the truth.

9-42: A persuasive speech by our President affects our opinions and arouses his critics.

9-43: People from Denmark have more sunstrokes than our African Americans do.

9-44: Don't try to sit on the fence.

9-45: Tickling babies will cause them to stutter.

9-46: If you stumble at the front door of your house, your home will experience bad luck.

9-47: A stranger is coming if a falling cup lands upright.

9-48: Sleep in a strange bed and your dream will come true.

9-49: Never trust a banker unless he or she is a family member.

9-50: Never fish near where the City dumps its sewage into the river.

Never serve evil men or women. Instead, move to another County.

CHAPTER TEN
ITEMS 1-50

10-1: Snowflakes of a small size means that a large winter storm is looming.

10-2: A cloud that grows taller promises more rain.

10-3: Wear two stockings of different colors and you will have a pleasant day.

10-4: For good luck, stir a pot with the right hand and in a clockwise manner.

10-5: Wear stockings with the wrong side out and you will be noticed.

10-6: Step on a person's grave and you will have bad luck.

10-7: When entering a home, always place the left foot forward.

10-8: Keep your back towards the mountains for more protection.

10-9: Don't feel blue and don't act red.

10-10: Let's have a stag party and watch each other intently.

10-11: Live in your own shell. Don't try to live in someone else's shell.

10-12: The fruit of his labor is not Hanes. It's called underwear.

10-13: Don't be full of boloney.

10-14: He was stewed to the gills.

10-15: She was stoned out of her gourd.

10-16: It's only a stone's throw away.

10-17: That was a straw man's match.

10-18: Practice what you preach.

10-19: She's as pretty as a picture.

10-20: She is prettier than her picture.

10-21: Pull up a chair.

10-22: Don't let them pull your string.

10-23: Put that in your meerschaum and smoke it.

10-24: Don't mind him, he is full of smoke.

10-25: She is funnier than a barrel of monkeys.

10-26: He was mad enough to hit the roof.

10-27: It's raining dewdrops and nothing more.

10-28: It's a rat race.

10-29: It's a race for rogues.

10-30: Life is the pits.

10-31: It's a piece of cake.

10-32: Nobody goes downhill forever.

10-33: You are a greenhorn only once.

10-34: The hand that rocks the cradle rules the World.

10-35: Grow roots someplace.

10-36: Don't play second fiddle.

10-37: If you live in a house with many windows, don't throw rocks at anyone.

10-38: Don't be a pig. Save some for the others.

10-39: Seek pearls, not swine.

10-40: Let's paint the town red.

10-41: He's a pain in the rear.

10-42: She's a pain to all of her former friends.

10-43: The handwriting is on the wall.

10-44: It's as plain as day.

10-45: It is as confusing as night.

10-46: That's a hung-dog situation.

10-47: Use a high chair only if you must.

10-48: A bridesmaid that stumbles at the altar will become an old maid.

10-49: A broom that falls upon the floor means that someone will soon die.

10-50: A horse fly inside of the house means that swatters will soon swing.

Show mercy toward those that do not know you for they may become your friends.

CHAPTER ELEVEN
ITEMS 1-50

11-1: Overcook cabbage to avoid digestion problems.

11-2: A slice of cake that falls on its side means bad luck.

11-3: A lighted candle must be placed near the head of a corpse to ward off evil spirits.

11-4: Cane sugar is sweeter than sugar made from beets.

11-5: If smoke rises straight into the air, it is a sign of good luck.

11-6: Stop playing cards if an ace falls upon the floor.

11-7: Carry a bible everywhere you go. You need to read it often.

11-8: If you need rain, water your tomatoes.

11-9: Never put on airs.

11-10: A small chin denotes cowardice.

11-11: Railroad men twist their overall straps for good luck.

11-12: Beware of a bare-footed woman.

11-13: If a squirrel crosses your path and heads toward the right, it is good luck.

11-14: When a star falls from the heavens above, make a wish and it will come true.

11-15: The higher that you develop in life, the harder you might fall as you get older.

11-16: It is almost like searching for a needle in a haystack.

11-17: We will cross that bridge when we get there.

11-18: Hit the sack, it is very late.

11-19: If the shoe fits, wear it.

11-20: A new broom should sweep clean.

11-21: Have a nightcap before retiring.

11-22: If the hat fits, wear it.

11-23: It is yours with no strings attached.

11-24: What happens behind closed doors is not your concern.

11-25: The best expression in WW-II was 'Nuts'.

11-26: Hitch your wagon to a rising star.

11-27: It was just another hole in the wall.

11-28: Don't be off your rocker.

11-29: He's over the hill.

11-30: It's a dog-eat-dog World.

11-31: If it isn't so, I will eat my hat.

11-32: Avoid women who don't wear any underwear.

11-33: One woman's meal is another woman's attraction.

11-34: One man's garbage is another man's wealth.

11-35: He didn't do anything wrong, he was framed.

11-36: A bull that's too old is left with an open pasture.

11-37: A man that is too old is left with unfulfilled desires.

11-38: Honesty is the best policy.

11-39: Always tell the truth and you won't have to remember what you said to whom.

11-40: If that's his story, he is really out on a limb.

11-41: Come on, why don't we call a spade a spade?

11-42: Imitation is the sincerest form of flattery.

11-43: Lean over backwards for me, please.

11-44: I am hungry enough to eat an entire deer.

11-45: Keep them in the dark if you can.

11-46: Life is a two-way street.

11-47: I was hung out to dry on that deal.

11-48: It's lost in my mind. But, give me five minutes and I will remember it.

11-49: It is hotter than a two-dollar pistol on a Saturday night.

11-50: A sun-bather may despise the rain, but, the farmer rarely will.

Don't bow down to politicians and, moreover, never serve them. If they come to your door, don't open it because, in the end, that will cost you money.

CHAPTER TWELVE
ITEMS 1-50

12-1: On this deal, you have me over the barrel.

12-2: Don't cry over milk that has been spilt.

12-3: Home is where you hang your hat.

12-4: Let the chips fall where they may.

12-5: It is a long and winding road from here to there.

12-6: Life is like a mountain with its ups and downs.

12-7: Home is sweeter when you are away from there.

12-8: A carriage without a horse never goes very far.

12-9: Gee, what a stew I am in.

12-10: You should not light the candle at both ends.

12-11: Don't kick the bucket before your time.

12-12: Too many men are like mushrooms because they grow up in the dark.

12-13: Now I am really in hot water.

12-14: Make hay while the sun shines.

12-15: The difference is like night and day.

12-16: A man's home is his castle.

12-17: Real men don't eat quiche.

12-18: The man who serves as his own doctor has a fool as his patient.

12-19: The man who serves as his own lawyer has a fool as a client.

12-20: The man who is self-taught has limited knowledge.

12-21: The child who is schooled at home misses too much.

12-22: You are lucky if lightning strikes elsewhere.

12-23: A woman without big knockers doesn't stand out.

12-24: If one is born during the Christmas season, that child will be gifted.

12-25: Relish the smaller pleasures most.

12-26: Avoid all lawyers at all costs.

12-27: If the sun shines through the branches of an apple tree on Christmas Day, there will be an abundant harvest for the next season.

12-28: Draw a circle on the ground to cause good luck.

12-29: When you are churning butter sing, "Come butter come" and the process will proceed more rapidly.

12-30: Wear old clothes for good luck.

12-31: The first star to be seen at night allows one wish that will come true.

12-32: Spit on fish bait if you want to catch more fish.

12-33: Drink sulfur and molasses in the Spring to bring good health.

12-34: Soap won't set unless it is made during a full moon.

12-35: A live spider in a shell around the neck wards off evil spirits.

12-36: Women aboard ship will bring bad luck to the ship.

12-37: An absent-minded Professor has forgotten more than most of his students will ever know.

12-38: Prosperity is always just around the corner.

12-39: If an animal has a thick fur, a long winter is coming.

12-40: Taking an umbrella with you will scare the rain away.

12-41: Walking in the rain while the Sun also shines suggests good luck.

12-42: Carry your rake with the teeth pointed upward.

12-43: Flipping a coin to a beggar brings good fortune to both.

12-44: Wise men know both the value and thickness of a penny.

12-45: If a wallet or a purse is given as a gift, it should contain some amount of money for good luck.

12-46: Having cold hands does suggest having a warm heart.

12-47: A warm spot on a seat cushion means that a woman has been there before you.

12-48: Dried coffee grounds from your Keurig machine will absorb a lot of grease.

12-49: Where there is smoke, there is fire.

12-50: A watched tea pot boils too slowly.

Never place your confidence in politicians even though he or she is of a high rank because, with them, there is no help for you and your problems.

CHAPTER THIRTEEN
ITEMS 1-50

13-1: A red ear of corn is an omen of good luck.

13-2: Crushed pine needles mixed with molasses are an efficient cough remedy.

13-3: If you pull on your finger and your joint cracks, you have recently told a lie.

13-4: If a cork is placed under your pillow, you won't have cramps.

13-5: A cotton string tied around the ankle will cure pain.

13-6: Transients commit more crimes than residents do.

13-7: Share your good fortune for even more wealth.

13-8: Cross-eyed people never do well in business.

13-9: Never trust anyone who wears sun glasses indoors.

13-10: If you have to tell a lie, keep your fingers crossed so that harm can be prevented.

13-11: If two people say the same thing at the same time, something good will happen to both.

13-12: Those that don't eat the crust of a pie are prone to lust.

13-13: Hooking two left and right little fingers together will make a wish come true.

13-14: When you are looking for something, why is it always at the last place where you look?

13-15: Wet the iron and you can expect rust.

13-16: If you hear the rooster crow, it will be a longer day.

13-17: Clean the tool and it will be clean when you need it.

13-18: Slices of onions placed on the chest cures lung infections.

13-19: An empty sack won't stay upright.

13-20: Say it like it is.

13-21: Bet only what you can afford to lose.

13-22: Live beneath your means.

13-23: Treat people as you want to be treated.

13-24: Don' learn the tricks of the trade. Instead, learn the trade.

13-25: Learn that all news is, to some degree, biased.

13-26: Be brave or, at least, pretend so.

13-27: Support at least one charity.

13-28: Never shut the door on a good opportunity.

13-29: Don't be cynical, be optimistic.

13-30: Love the best pleasures longer.

13-31: Use credit cards for your convenience, not for loading up your credit.

13-32: Walk two miles at a brisk pace each day.

13-33: Smiles cost very little but they mean so much.

13-34: Read and understand the Bible.

13-35: Learn to listen and listen to learn.

13-36: Never open a door without knocking.

13-37: Keep your timepiece fast and be early for appointments.

13-38: Insufficient money is just a temporary problem.

13-39: Always leave the toilet seat in the down position.

13-40: Never go to the outhouse without a corn cob or a piece of newspaper.

13-41: If provoked, don't respond until next day.

13-42: Skip one meal each week.

13-43: Diplomacy and tact are the highways to success.

13-44: Speak softly but always have a defense plan in your mind.

13-45: If you must fight, hit first and hit as hard as you can.

13-46: Payback is fair play.

13-47: People create their own mess.

13-48: Living in suburbia is nice until you consider your long commute.

13-49: Be tough minded but soft spoken.

13-50: Don't try to sway the opinions of narrow-minded bigots.

Lift up your thoughts onto the hills of Hazard from which I came. That will give you grace just as it was given to me many long years ago.

CHAPTER FOURTEEN
ITEMS 1-50

14-1: It is better to have new ideas than to collect old facts.

14-2: Be kinder than you need to be.

14-3: Never make the same mistake twice.

14-4: In business, make no assumptions.

14-5: Know that the larger font size draws what the smaller font size repels.

14-6: Ignore that which you are unable to transform.

14-7: Treat your wife as your best friend.

14-8: Know what you stand for and what you stand against.

14-9: Be curious and ask good questions.

14-10: Give your kids the best.

14-11: Give people what they want more than anything else. Give them your appreciation.

14-12: Show respect for all life forms.

14-13: Nothing is as important as it first seems.

14-14: Get better, not older.

14-15: Profit by your errors.

14-16: Question who is right versus what is right.

14-17: Never let a minor become your major.

14-18: Don't burden a buddy with bull shit.

14-19: Praise in public but, criticize in private.

14-20: Never tell a man how tired he appears.

14-21: Never tell a lady how old she looks.

14-22: If we lose a war, pray that we might win the peace.

14-23: First impressions don't last very long.

14-24: Promise much but deliver more.

14-25: Always look for the best in a person. Don't waste time looking for the worst.

14-26: Be humble. A lot was done before your time.

14-27: Associate with people that look for solutions, not those that search for problems.

14-28: Beware of any person who has too little to lose.

14-29: Leave every place cleaner than you first found it to be.

14-30: The farmer who makes the soil better than when he first bought it will always have the best harvest.

14-31: A business deal isn't over until the check clears all of the banks.

14-32: Don't burn your bridges. You may need to go that way again.

14-33: Problems are nothing more than opportunities.

14-34: Life is fair and unfair. It's a matter of judgment.

14-35: Disagree without being disagreeable.

14-36: Envy is the source of much grief.

14-37: We are each given the same amount of time to do something worthy. Each day we are all allowed a total of 24-hours.

14-38: Have a good idea? Act before others do.

14-39: Winners do what losers cannot.

14-40: Seek opportunity, not security.

14-41: A higher price doesn't always mean a better product.

14-42: Bigger is not always better.

14-43: Buy the best that you can afford.

14-44: There is only one word that describes a successful career and that is called work.

14-45: Be there when needed.

14-46: Be decisive, not derisive.

14-47: No one should try to make it alone.

14-48: Do business with those who do business with you.

14-49: Feel good about yourself.

14-50: Always try to develop a better attitude.

Happy and successful is he or she who gets their support from above.
And, it is proper to sing praises on God's behalf.

CHAPTER FIFTEEN
ITEMS 1-50

15-1: Let one day a week be a family day where everyone votes and the majority rules.

15-2: Handle details before they bite you by the tail.

15-3: Be a self-starter and a big-mover.

15-4: Possessions break more relationships than they make.

15-5: Pay your own way.

15-6: Make things better, not bigger.

15-7: Possessions must never be allowed to possess you.

15-8: Never apologize for success.

15-9: Do what must be done today, not tomorrow.

15-10: Your best asset is your reputation.

15-11: Don't wallow in self-pity.

15-12: Do more than that which is required.

15-13: Performance profits from a constructive attitude.

15-14: Everyone learns more if we each listen more closely.

15-15: A sense of humor doesn't cure anything but it doesn't hurt anything either.

15-16: Don't compromise your integrity.

15-17: Use your time for action, not for useless words.

15-18: Don't try to rain on other people's parade.

15-19: Be like a scout, be prepared.

15-20: Best advice begins by setting a good example.

15-21: Finish whatever you begin.

15-22: A good boss makes decisions quickly but a better boss encourages others to work more efficiently.

15-23: Out of sight becomes out of mind.

15-24: Those who are absent from a meeting always get the blame.

15-25: A rich man that wants to understand more must live some of his life as a poor man.

15-26: One profits very little in the near term by sowing seeds.

15-27: Abuse is the weapon of the wicked.

15-28: A stopped clock is correct twice in each day.

15-29: Don't gaze at the distance. Focus on what is closer.

15-30: Action enhances life. Inaction makes life miserable.

15-31: Become important to someone.

15-32: Know that the itch gets the scratch.

15-33: Too much scratching brings blood.

15-34: Learn to improve what you want to admire.

15-35: A declining Nation is one without enough adventure or resources.

15-36: Dare naught and need more.

15-37: Adversity builds character.

15-38: Prosperity teaches much but, adversity teaches more.

15-39: Washington DC has become a place that gives too much advice and too little help.

15-40: The road towards a place where help is needed begins with a single step.

15-41: Affection is never wasted on people.

15-42: An aged behavior is, too often, a developed one.

15-43: When old age exists, wisdom is ever-present.

15-44: One cannot have the ocean without its noise.

15-45: You learn very little from those who always agree with you.

15-46: If two politicians voice the same opinion, one is a liar.

15-47: It is more gratifying to fail at something large than something small.

15-48: The future belongs to he who waxes more eloquently.

15-49: If it is to be, then it is left to thee.

15-50: Great projects attract great minds.

Don't trust princes, politicians or parrots because they will never help you.

CHAPTER SIXTEEN
ITEMS 1-50

16-1: We grow too small in trying to be too great.

16-2: Successful writers have readers and unsuccessful writers use a Vanity Press.

16-3: Unsuccessful authors have lazy agents.

16-4: Too much ambition impedes success.

16-5: Begin at the bottom to reach the top.

16-6: Do not view America as a union of different states. America is the United States.

16-7: The best gift is a good nature toward all others.

16-8: Ignorance about a few things is acceptable but ignorance about all things is absolutely inexcusable.

16-9: A man's amusements can reveal his true character traits.

16-10: Life is worth living if we avoid most temptations.

16-11: Genealogy is tough work. You have to work awfully hard to find a good ancestor.

16-12: Man develops his own future but he inherits his parents.

16-13: The best part of any family lies under the ground.

16-14: The credit of being well bred belongs to your parents.

16-15: Anger without cause is repulsive to others.

16-16: It is madness to expect success before its time.

16-17: The best fears to have are those that are never felt.

16-18: If you must face misfortunes, don't share them with your friends.

16-19: We are too often governed by our appearances.

16-20: Never condemn someone for having a beard. He is probably hiding something.

16-21: Be what you can be, especially while others are watching.

16-22: Most of the hard work is done by those with the smallest salary.

16-23: If a person walks, talks and acts like a dummy, then that person is probably dumb.

16-24: Two of life's greatest problems are these: (1) Why logic cannot prevail and (2) Why appetites won't listen to reason.

16-25: Some of us eat to live while others live to eat.

16-26: Behind every argument is someone's bias.

16-27: The best way to lose friends is to win arguments.

16-28: Hard work creates facts, not fiction.

16-29: A long feud means that both families are at fault.

16-30: People quarrel when they don't know how to argue.

16-31: Aristocrats love freedom but they hate equality.

16-32: Love and education will disarm most barriers.

16-33: Learning and knowing are exercises for both teacher and student. But, the better a student becomes, the better things are for both.

16-34: Art is but an image of reality.

16-35: The extreme form of censorship is called murder.

16-36: Bad people survive because it is against the law to kill them.

16-37: A Christian is a person whose support mechanisms are invisible.

16-38: Wise leaders use authority in a responsible manner.

16-39: In Germany, it is against the law to point the middle finger upward at someone.

16-40: Workers don't need to take their worries home to wives and family. Instead, they do need to take home all of their paycheck to their wives and children.

16-41: As wealth increases, greed also increases.

16-42: A person that is too greedy will always be poorer than he or she wants to be.

16-43: We were the richest family on Combs Street. Our problem was that we didn't have much money.

16-44: The average student works harder than the 'A' student.

16-45: Not doing more than most will keep the average down.

16-46: An average jury contains twelve locals of typical ignorance.

16-47: Every new baby gives new hope that the World will prosper as a result of his birth.

16-48: The worst part about new babies is the silly parents.

16-49: All new people begin in like manner, as babies.

16-50: Unmarried men pretend to know women best and unmarried women pretend to know men best.

Show gracious behavior and steadfast love to all of your family and you will receive much more in return.

CHAPTER SEVENTEEN
ITEMS 1-50

17-1: It ought to be a law that all young people should become married.

17-2: A bachelor is called a boy forever but, an unmarried woman is called an old maid.

17-3: It is your smile that thee does best.

17-4: A bargain should be those items which the store is losing money on.

17-5: Too often a person pays more and gets less.

17-6: A husband's lament: "See how much money I saved, honey."

17-7: Beauty does not create or destroy, it merely transforms.

17-8: Beauty is not created for everyone, it either exists or it doesn't.

17-9: Nothing is beautiful in every way.

17-10: Beauty is skin deep and it is one of skin's greatest assets.

17-11: Behavior should be the mirror of our image.

17-12: Behave well while others around you behave badly.

17-13: Too often, what is best believed is least understood.

17-14: Beauty is what a woman gets too early and loses too soon.

17-15: Be nice to people early in your career because you might need their support later on.

17-16: Why is it easier to accept than to challenge?

17-17: Beliefs should create reasons not treason.

17-18: Terrorists are cowards who are afraid to do anything positive.

17-19: One person with a strong constructive belief is worth thousands who only possess an interest.

17-20: If you believe in nothing, take time to believe the Bible.

17-21: Learned persons have to be careful or they might become bigots.

17-22: There is some truth and a little virtue in every issue.

17-23: People that shouldn't have children sometimes do.

17-24: If Mother Nature had somehow decreed that both men and women could take turns at giving birth, the maximum family size would be four.

17-25: Abortion qualifies as premeditated murder.

17-26: One blessing for the blind is that they don't have to contend with mirrors.

17-27: The blindest of all are those who can see but, look upon others without sensitivity.

17-28: Love may be blind but hatred is more blind.

17-29: Too often, blood is what people try to ignore the most.

17-30: A lasting peace means that blood will be spilled later on.

17-31: A maiden's blush can be an important attribute.

17-32: A healthy soul can survive in a sick body but a sick soul cannot long endure in a healthy body.

17-33: Be bonded, not bound.

17-34: The greatest challenge in life is how to live in our own skin.

17-35: Misfortune befriends the meek.

17-36: If you are overly concerned about the fall, you will never know the thrill of the rise.

17-37: Heroes try to do what cowards won't.

17-38: Given the choice, choose the bolder.

17-39: Do your duty, soldier.

17-40: The best books are opened with anticipation and closed with more knowledge.

17-41: One who never reads qualifies as an illiterate.

17-42: The better books are those that make the readers think.

17-43: A good home shelters both body and mind.

17-44: Books and friends have much in common, both are chosen.

17-45: A boring person is one who talks too much and listens too little.

17-46: One cannot communicate well without saying something swell.

17-47: Writers should never wed. There isn't enough time for both.

17-48: The men that complain about money too much are those that have the least.

17-49: It is easy to be a bore and it is harder to avoid being one.

17-50: A bore is a person who is inclined to turn a conversation into a monologue.

Teach me to do better so that I may improve. But, teach me to do worse and I will never survive.

CHAPTER EIGHTEEN
ITEMS 1-50

18-1: A borrower who pays his debt is socially acceptable but a beggar who can't pay his debt is never socially accepted.

18-2: Those that try to borrow in order to cover every mistake that they ever made will regret both the amount that they borrowed and all the days that follow.

18-3: There are just two classes of people at the end of the day, borrowers and lenders.

18-4: There are just two kinds of people, the doers and the watchers.

18-5: You should lead, follow or eat dust.

18-6: One who borrows does not have all of his freedoms.

18-7: Bankers have excellent recall.

18-8: Never borrow money on your house. You could become homeless.

18-9: Little boys grow up to become bigger boys.

18-10: Men are boys between their birth and until their death.

18-11: Fathers rarely understand their sons well enough.

18-12: A son can leave his home without caring enough.

18-13: A son's former home must be a remembered thing.

18-14: The more testimony that is given, the less that is remembered.

18-15: Say less and profit more.

18-16: In speech classes, the ultimate goal is to learn brevity.

18-17: The fewer the words, the more successful is the request.

18-18: Eloquence can reside where brevity should live.

18-19: Our World is too small to support isolationists.

18-20: Our World is too fragile to support terrorists.

18-21: Mankind will not long survive without more brotherhood.

18-22: If every Negro decides to marry within his own race, how will that help us to ever become brothers?

18-23: Sub-divisions are aptly named. They offer fine homes that are divided by bigots who narrow a neighborhood without broadening the brotherhood.

18-24: It is more convenient to love mankind than to love the family that lives next door.

18-25: During the day, love thy neighbor. But, at night, bolt the door and load your pistol. Home invasions are occurring at a record-high incident rate.

18-26: Drink Sassafras tea for sore eyes.

18-27: Grease your feet to ward off head colds.

18-28: Use river mud for insect bites.

18-29: To kill a wart, rub it daily with an Indian head penny.

18-30: Eat lots of watermelon to reduce a fever.

18-31: After a person dies, open all of the doors and windows so that the spirit can rise.

18-32: People with dimpled chins don't commit murder.

18-33: Drop a dishrag and your sweetheart will soon appear.

18-34: When a dog eats grass, rain is coming.

18-35: A modern choice: Live at your parent's home or perish together as idiots.

18-36: Be a good master so that your pet won' bite you.

18-37: Fresh peach twigs make the best dousing rods.

18-38: If you talk about dreams before breakfast is finished, those dreams won't come true.

18-39: For good luck, approach a water fountain from the East, not the West.

18-40: If your ear burns, someone is talking about you.

18-41: If you hear a ringing sound in your ears, news is coming your way.

18-42: Large ears suggest a generous nature.

18-43: Long ears suggest a long life.

18-44: Pierced ears will keep demons away.

18-45: For good luck, wear three new things on Easter morning.

18-46: If you miss your mouth and cause food to fall to the floor, bad luck is headed in your direction.

18-47: If someone glares at you, it brings bad luck.

18-48: Seven is the number for good luck but, eight is the number that brings misfortune.

18-49: Never allow a chair to be vacant at a formal dinner. That causes bad luck.

18-50: Sleep with a book under your pillow if you desire more wisdom.

Train your mind for war and your hands for battle and, maybe, the Afghanistan Rebels will retreat more often.

CHAPTER NINETEEN
ITEMS 1-50

19-1: Two eyebrows that grow together as one drives people away.

19-2: Never trust a person with green eyes.

19-3: Peacock feathers keep sick people alive longer.

19-4: Being born on February the 29th is a sign of good luck.

19-5: Mend your fences before trouble begins.

19-6: If you see a pretty handkerchief on the ground, leave it there. Don't pick it up or you will inherit a reason to start crying.

19-7: The best liars have short fingernails.

19-8: If a firefly enters the house, the number of people in that household will change by one during the following day.

19-9: If a piece of burning coal spews out of the fireplace and onto the hearth, company is coming.

19-10: All business deals involve risk.

19-11: Nothing is guaranteed in life but death.

19-12: Change is the only thing in life that is constant.

19-13: A little cuddle will ward off a lot of trouble.

19-14: Hug, don't mug.

19-15: Fire strikes thrice as lightening does.

19-16: Heart attacks give two warnings before the killing one appears.

19-17: Friends usually don't remain friends if they work together.

19-18: If you get choked on food, hold your arms as high as you can and have someone pull very hard on your big toe.

19-19: Busy people are too busy to take time to cry.

19-20: If you are fishing on the river bank, don't let pigs or Baptist preachers get too close.

19-21: To have fun, we need to stay occupied and be employed.

19-22: A flea on your back means that you owe someone money.

19-23: Think too much about hard times and you will soon endure them.

19-24: If you pick fruit before it is ripe, you will get a sty on your eye.

19-25: The best test of true character is called danger.

19-26: What was said is far more important than who said it.

19-27: Never re-fold your napkin. That brings bad luck.

19-28: It is wise to be candid.

19-29: Playing with a cat will cause bad health.

19-30: Always fold paper money in a direction that is toward yourself.

19-31: Capital is wealth that creates more wealth.

19-32: A just cause will eventually succeed.

19-33: Don't refrigerate food in a can. Use a glass jar.

19-34: Live humble but die noble.

19-35: It's bad luck to go back inside of a house to retrieve something that has been forgotten.

19-36: Where important issues are concerned, it is not important whether you win or lose. What matters most is your support.

19-37: If you forget something while you are speaking, it means that you are telling lies.

19-38: Let the eyes be efficient while the tongue takes a break.

19-39: Wisest sight is hindsight.

19-40: Anything that contains the number four should be held sacred.

19-41: Too many precautions will cause too much fear.

19-42: Learn from the mistakes of others.

19-43: If a girl eats a four leaf clover, she will marry the first bachelor that she meets.

19-44: Dangerous words are spoken most by those who are suppressed.

19-45: Every book teaches something.

19-46: Freckles can be removed by rubbing the face with a wet frog.

19-47: If abortion had always been popular, we might not have had the pleasure of knowing Jesus.

19-48: Criticism is the price that we pay for success.

19-49: A trip begun on Friday will never be successful.

19-50: If two people poke a fire at the same time, they will soon argue with each other.

Give ear to my voice when I call for you and things will be fine
between the two of us.

CHAPTER TWENTY
ITEMS 1-50

20-1: Shooting holes in a man's boat will attract demons.

20-2: Turning over garbage cans will alert the police.

20-3: Black cats should wear warning bells and walk only in small circles.

20-4: Two people should never wash their hands in the same basin at the same time. That brings bad luck.

20-5: Fever blisters are caused by a dirty toothbrush.

20-6: People that eat too fast have more cankers.

20-7: Rejection always encourages acceptance.

20-8: If a fruit tree is barren, it needs a nail.

20-9: To know everything about one thing is to know too little about almost everything else.

20-10: Kill a frog and the cow will give bad milk.

20-11: One certainty is that everything else might be uncertain.

20-12: Sex is like a foreign language. If you don't use it, you lose it.

20-13: The common denominator is death.

20-14: Don't count the number of cars in a funeral procession. It is unlucky to do so.

20-15: Take off your hat in the presence of women or cadavers.

20-16: Garlic hung around the house will ward off evil spirits.

20-17: Change for the sake of change is improper and unacceptable.

20-18: When you get out of bed, face the North as soon as possible.

20-19: Those who refuse to try new things will always have old problems.

20-20: Never sing until after breakfast is over.

20-21: He who cannot change himself will never change the World.

20-22: Nothing stays exactly the same.

20-23: After dark, cemeteries should be left to the dead.

20-24: Don't sit upon a tombstone. It brings bad luck.

20-25: If you read this entire book, luck will mean much more to you.

20-26: He or she who lives life best is better prepared for death.

20-27: All of us are accountable for our own character.

20-28: If you want to know people better, study them, don't just look at them.

20-29: Use a coffee mug only for coffee and the coffee will always taste better.

20-30: Never wash your coffee mug. The soap and water will affect the taste.

20-31: Never give gloves as a gift. People will always think poorly of you for doing so.

20-32: Defective character traits are not easily mended.

20-33: Best character traits will always surface after the worst crisis appears.

20-34: Goldfish bring bad luck.

20-35: A five dollar gold piece should be given only to children.

20-36: Break glass on Good Friday for good luck.

20-37: In the presence of older adults, children must be seen and not heard.

20-38: The sun never shines on meatless Tuesday.

20-39: The eating of turkey on Thanksgiving Day brings good fortune.

20-40: The man who insists on eating ham on Thanksgiving Day is either bent or unique.

20-41: Berry seeds cause appendicitis or gall bladder problems.

20-42: A grave should always face toward the East.

20-43: Read too many epitaphs and you will lose your memory.

20-44: Not all gypsies are gyps.

20-45: Make the best of yourself because that should be your favorite workpiece.

20-46: Good citizenship requires three I's which are initiative, imagination and individuality.

20-47: People who grind their teeth at night have worms.

20-48: Growing pains are to be endured if the child is to become an adult.

20-49: Too often, charity begins at home. The problem is that, on too many occasions, it stays there.

20-50: Those who give more are the richest.

Where shall I go from here? Will I ascend to Heaven or will I descend toward the wicked one down below?

CHAPTER TWENTY-ONE
ITEMS 1-50

21-1: He who waits to achieve the greatest deed ever will always wait.

21-2: Search for the need, not the root cause.

21-3: Fright turns the hair white.

21-4: Eat bread crumbs if you want curly hair.

21-5: Long hair on the back of your hands predicts a large fortune.

21-6: Every gracious act is a down-payment for Heaven.

21-7: Real heart trouble is to have an attitude that is heartless.

21-8: Give much to receive more.

21-9: Those that enjoy giving the most were, at one time, very poor themselves.

21-10: Widows and widowers have the worst hair problems.

21-11: Anything green is supposed to bring good luck.

21-12: Rub smooth wood for a continued spell of good luck.

21-13: If you shake hands with a politician, wash your hands afterwards.

21-14: Never let a politician kiss your baby.

21-15: A cross that is hung on the outside of the house will ward off evil.

21-16: A swarm of bugs or bees is always an ill omen.

21-17: A person that is too plain will never know true happiness.

21-18: The greatest charm is a cheerful attitude.

21-19: A house without laughter cannot become a better home.

21-20: Cheer to be cheered.

21-21: Women who were not virgins when they got married don't want to talk about that.

21-22: A hat that is placed under the bed will bring bad luck.

21-23: Absence makes the heart grow fonder and the reunion more intense.

21-24: Before it can become worse, it has to get better.

21-25: A charming personality is more important than additional beauty.

21-26: In any marriage, two people can see too much of each other.

21-27: A hem that will not stay flat means a new boyfriend will soon appear.

21-28: Hex signs will ward off evil spirits.

21-29: Children should not be treated as angels.

21-30: Why are men permitted a second childhood but only one youth?

21-31: If you want people to be good, make them happy.

21-32: Offspring make the man.

21-33: The scourge of youth is called potential.

21-34: Most of the honesty in this World is owned by the youngest of our children.

21-35: Our most valuable resource is our people.

21-36: Show every child some kindness.

21-37: Kids are bad luck only after they grow up.

21-38: Moonshine is a good tonic for rheumatism.

21-39: A gray horse at the track will bring higher earnings at the gambling booth.

21-40: Good children make a poor man rich.

21-41: Spit on your little finger and rub it on an oak tree for good luck.

21-42: To calm a little girl, brush her hair.

21-43: To calm a little boy, rub his back.

21-44: Choose the path of good, not evil.

21-45: Thank God that we cannot have everything.

21-46: A cat with one white leg is to be avoided.

21-47: The bigger the hoof, the stronger the horse.

21-48: Hang a horseshoe with the open end up to maintain good luck.

21-49: There is too much evil and too little good.

21-50: Christianity abounds among terminally-ill patients.

Those who can be trusted best by me are the men and women of a mountain town because I have so much in common with each of them.

CHAPTER TWENTY-TWO
ITEMS 1-50

22-1: Never build a barn exactly where the burned barn once stood.

22-2: Touch a handicapped person for good luck.

22-3: Weak minds are easily swayed. Don't take advantage of them.

22-4: It's bad luck to start a project without finishing it.

22-5: The last board is more quickly nailed into its position.

22-6: It brings bad luck to kill a lady bug.

22-7: If March begins like a lamb, it will end like a lion.

22-8: If April has no showers, pity the poor flowers of May. You may have to wait until next year.

22-9: Never get married during the months that have days of equal length, during March or September.

22-10: Marry during the month with the longest day, marry in June.

22-11: Have your babies in the shortest month, February.

22-12: Marriage vows sworn in May will soon be broken.

22-13: Rain on a wedding day brings bad luck.

22-14: June 3rd is the luckiest marriage date of all.

22-15: In terms of persuasion, the mind is no match for the heart.

22-16: Our own faults must be addressed before any others are considered.

22-17: As comforts increase, complaints may also increase.

22-18: People that complain too much have more to explain.

22-19: An employee who makes the most noise is the first to be replaced.

22-20: Manage your workstation like a submarine, run silent and run deep.

22-21: One who hears best knows more.

22-22: Compliments must be earned.

22-23: Know when to say just enough.

22-24: Tell people that they are not like all the others.

22-25: Beer every night can mean a headache every morning.

22-26: If you measure the size of your hands, expect hard times.

22-27: People who eat red meat have a bad temper.

22-28: Most of the meat that you eat is never digested.

22-29: The hillbilly diet uses meat, potatoes, biscuits and milk gravy. On occasions, it was changed to milk gravy, biscuits, potatoes and meat.

22-30: The man with a bald head is rarely forgetful.

22-31: What must be memorized for school is always better done when it is memorized before breakfast is begun.

22-32: Teachers are expected to be the best students in the classroom. If not, something is wrong with the system.

22-33: The attorneys that need much and want more may actually have less.

22-34: Bend if you must but, try to stay unbroken.

22-35: The weaker ones understand compromise best.

22-36: In Washington DC, politicians agree with each other but never with the President.

22-37: In Washington DC, compromise should be the way of life but, confrontation exists more often than not.

22-38: I like business best when we are without those nasty little recessions.

2-39: Life is great in between hard times.

22-40: Compromise does not alter human rights, it makes them better.

22-41: A better life requires more education.

22-42: One must leave a house by the same door in which he entered.

22-43: If both eyes itch, your ancestors are admiring your work.

22-44: The loss of a favorite umbrella will bring bad luck.

22-45: Never pick up a lost umbrella or you will have more bad luck.

22-46: Being humble gains more than being clever does.

22-47: It may be smart to be clever but, being too clever is never wise.

22-48: Good ideas are taken to a meeting where they are sometimes destroyed.

22-49: Common sense is uncommon these days.

22-50: Liars avoid eye contact.

I lift up my eyes unto the hills from whence I came and I have feelings, fondness and good faith for all of my teachers who helped me so much.

CHAPTER TWENTY-THREE
ITEMS 1-50

23-1: See something as it is, not as you prefer it to be.

23-2: If two letters by an agent and a writer pass each other in the postal system, one of those letters will bring disappointing news.

23-3: Some lice on the head needs to be cracked before going to bed.

23-4: Lilac petals are easily swallowed if good fortune exists.

23-5: Lips that itch means that someone wants to kiss you.

23-6: Gifted people need to use their gifts.

23-7: Wise men have long since given up the habit of excessive speech.

23-8: Good conversation requires better listening.

23-9: Good decisions should be based upon what one needs instead of what one wants.

23-10: Communism offers three elements and those are poverty, hunger and envy.

23-11: Numbers ending in 3, 7, 9 and 12 bring good luck.

23-12: My luckiest number is 711 taken from the house number that I spent my youthful days and nights in.

23-13: Love and lust mean different things and it is wrong to think that they are identical.

23-14: For true love, just be true to your mate.

23-15: It is better to lucky than wise.

23-16: A mole near the mouth indicates good luck.

23-17: A wart on the arm indicates great strength.

23-18: A wart between your toes demands that you change your socks each morning.

23-19: People who handle eggs have more warts.

23-20: More moles indicate a greater wealth.

23-21: Moles on women are called beauty marks.

23-22: A confession by one benefits many.

23-23: A confession by an innocent person is more often one that is forced by the police.

23-24: A confession by an innocent person can be staged to protect the one that he loves.

23-25: Good work begins where bad work ends.

23-26: They that can succeed always thought that they could.

23-27: If you have done a small thing well, you can do a large thing better.

23-28: Trust only yourself so that no person can betray you.

23-29: Prosperity exists when everybody tries harder.

23-30: Once something new is made, it is no longer new.

23-31: Young people are nice since they have not yet been corrupted by life.

23-32: One must march to his own music.

23-33: Old authors don't write any better than the younger ones but, they do erase more.

23-34: There is safety in numbers.

23-35: Look where the herd is heading and go with the herd.

23-36: Don't follow a herd too much. That could lead you to a slaughter house.

23-37: It is exciting to take risks.

23-38: It is hard to corrupt a good conscience.

23-39: If you are lucky, conscience arrives shortly after birth and remains with you until you are dead.

23-40: Never go gently into a bad night.

23-41: Avoid the big sleep for as long as you can.

23-42: Strive to stay alive.

23-43: Get hugs, not drugs.

23-44: Think, don't drink.

23-45: Alcohol is the ultimate spot remover. Alcohol removes you from your rightful spot.

23-46: Addiction is a form of slavery.

23-47: A two dollar bill is seldom circulated. Instead, it is hoarded as a prized possession.

23-48: If the moon shines on the closed eyelids of a sleeper, that sleeper will have bad dreams.

23-49: Lunacy is not caused by too much moon light. It is more often caused by badly-brewed moonshine.

23-50: Gather herbs before the full moon arrives.

I love the law and my son-in-law who is a policeman. Without his help, a lot of carpetbaggers would have fleeced me out of what little I own or possess.

CHAPTER TWENTY-FOUR
ITEMS 1-50

24-1: Take your medicine during a full moon for the maximum effect.

24-2: Bacon that curls in the skillet was killed at the wrong time of the year.

24-3: Never look at the moon over your left shoulder. That's bad luck.

24-4: Always over cook pork. That's the best way to avoid eating round worms.

24-5: More crimes are committed during a full moon.

24-6: Point your middle finger at the moon for good luck.

24-7: Never go into the moonlight without several coins in your pocket or purse.

24-8: If moon rays are seen between tall trees, life will be kind for you.

24-9: Game that is hunted at night during a full moon will be tainted by evil spirits.

24-10: Be superior, not inferior.

24-11: Be better than you need to be.

24-12: You get what you pay for.

24-13: Learn how to enjoy what you have.

24-14: Wish upon the stars but, never upon the moon.

24-15: Charred stones mark hallowed ground.

24-16: Never extinguish a fire with urine. Those two together make a horrible odor.

24-17: Bait traps or fishing hands while you are wearing gloves so that your scent will go undetected by the fish or game. This is an old trick used by people that smoke cigarettes and have yellow fingers.

24-18: Never be content with what you are or what you were. Worry about what you can be.

24-19: To be content can mean that you have given up on becoming better. Don't let that happen.

24-20: Know what is sufficient for anything and zoom in, not out.

24-21: Be satisfied with a little but, always, want more.

24-22: Be happy with what you have accomplished and you will accomplish less in the future.

24-23: If you cannot get what you want, want what you can get.

24-24: Be a big duck in a little pond or be a little duck in a large pond.

24-25: In strong light, always cast a long shadow.

24-26: Joy and grief are like sunshine and rain, one always follows the other.

24-27: Happiness exists where sorrow is absent.

24-28: The most successful language is called silence.

24-29: Conceit causes more trouble than wisdom does.

24-30: On moving day, keep a loaf of bread and a dash of salt nearby for good luck.

24-31: One's own taste in music may not please the others.

24-32: Classical music sweeps the mind clean.

24-33: Never step on a rusty nail.

24-34: Never walk the Kentucky River bed without tough shoes.

24-35: A pedicure and ice cream represents the great life.

24-36: A nail biter is always hungry or very nervous.

24-37: In today's society, you can run but you cannot hide.

24-38: You can change your name if you are a Hollywood actor but, not much else will change.

24-39: The rarest sentence in a conversation between two College Professors is, "I do not know."

24-40: The biggest word in our language is the tiny word, "if".

24-41: Our country will endure until our citizens are no longer willing to fight for it.

24-42: Washington DC will continue to exist until the money disappears. And, when that happens, they will be followed by an angry bunch of headhunters with hunting knives.

24-43: If you can't always be right, don't always be wrong.

24-44: If you must endure defeat, do it without losing faith or face.

24-45: Don't be concerned about your death. That's beyond your realm of influence to control.

24-46: To have courage is to put fear aside.

24-47: Keep your chimney clean of ash, just in case.

24-48: I'd like to meet the man who can eat only one potato chip.

24-49: Self-control is demonstrated by a man who can eat just one slice of Havarti cheese.

24-50: If the first person that a Caucasian sees on New Year's Day is black, then the entire year will be lucky for both parties. They should hug each other and give thanks.

Allow me to understand the way of my enemies and I will make them disappear.

CHAPTER TWENTY-FIVE
ITEMS 1-50

25-1: Try to walk a better path on every New Year's Day.

25-2: Always bring something new to a house on New Year's Day.

25-3: Count nine stars for nine successive nights and your wish will be granted.

25-4: String beans should be hung over the kitchen door for good luck.

25-5: Never grow a garden near the outhouse.

25-6: If there is a creek nearby, build your outhouse downstream and try to live at the head of the hollow.

25-7: At one time, minced ham was called 'round steak' and wieners were called 'tube steak'.

25-8: If you live in the country, be kind to your water well.

25-9: If you must have an outside toilet, dig the deepest one that you can afford.

25-10: Use old newspapers for wallpaper on your outside toilet so that your children may learn to read.

25-11: If you live close to the railroad tracks, learn to live with the noise and the ground that shakes.

25-12: An itchy nose means that someone close is angry at you.

25-13: When peeling onions, place a large toothpick between your teeth to avoid any burning of the eyes.

25-14: The hoot of an owl means that some young girl has lost her virginity.

25-15: A howling wolf means that an ancient spirit is unhappy.

25-16: A region that has no sounds at night has been desecrated so badly that the ancient spirits have been banished elsewhere.

25-17: Never allow bird feathers to be placed inside of the house.

25-18: A ring set with a pearl will bring tears to the owner.

25-19: If you can peel an entire apple without ever breaking the peeling, you will have good luck throughout the day.

25-20: A courtroom is where confusing matters are made more confusing.

25-21: There is no justice other than the different degrees of injustice.

25-22: Jurors are told to think but, not to talk. That is why so many jurors fall asleep on the job.

25-23: One form of entertainment is called jury duty.

25-24: Lawyers and criminals spend too much time together. Eventually, they both behave in a similar manner.

25-25: It costs very little to show some courtesy.

25-26: There is always room for better manners.

25-27: Wisely choose the words that you use and you will become more polite over time.

25-28: Tread lightly except for adversaries.

25-29: Some arrogant heroes would rather face bullets than criticisms.

25-30: Creation begins with one idea.

25-31: Generally, Old Army heroes are satisfied with the past, but discontent with the present and unsure about the future.

25-32: Women would prefer dead heroes over live cowards.

25-33: Fear can be used to motivate men but, cowardice cannot.

25-34: A coward knows what ought to be done but, he won't do what needs to be done.

25-35: One miscarriage of justice is called an abortion.

25-36: A cowardly approach won't win a single prize.

25-37: Most cowards and dogs have much in common. Their bark is worse than their bite.

25-38: Mountain men are not afraid of heights.

25-39: If you are served black-eyed peas, you know that Kentucky is to the North. If you are served pinto beans, you know that Tennessee is toward the South.

25-40: Never wear black gemstones to a party. Wear them only to funerals.

25-41: Real men eat potatoes, not rice.

25-42: Girls who can't keep hairpins in their hair will always suffer from anxiety.

25-43: Find an Indian-head penny and you are going to be wealthy.

25-44: Never expect any thanks for a plant which is given as a gift. Someone has to dig a hole, don't they?

25-45: Too much fertilizer will produce more blossoms than fruit.

25-46: Eat a raw pumpkin and suffer the itch.

25-47: Pumpkins and carrots are said to be good for the eyes.

25-48: Thin fur on an animal means that a long summer is due.

25-49: The blood of all races is not identical.

25-50: Rats that leave a home bestow bad luck upon that residence.

Blessed are those who do no harm to others and walk in rightful ways.

CHAPTER TWENTY-SIX
ITEMS 1-50

26-1: Red-haired women should never churn milk.

26-2: Redheads are usually hotheads.

26-3: Redheads make the best sauerkraut.

26-4: Too often, redheads know the devil too well.

26-5: One redhead in a family of black-haired people suggests than a grievous sin has been committed.

26-6: A lost-then-found thimble is a sign of good luck.

26-7: Wear the color white if you want to have good luck.

26-8: If you prick your finger while sewing, be certain to keep the bloodstain off of the article that is being sewn. Otherwise, the owner of the bloodstained article will experience much misfortune.

26-9: As the family goes, so goes the Nation.

26-10: Altars exert a strange affect. Altars do alter the ways of men and women.

26-11: A happy home is a wonderful thing to possess.

26-12: Some men may not fight for their Country but, most men will defend their own home. Beware of this, all of you home invaders.

26-13: Government needs to abide by the same rules that families have to follow.

26-14: It is hardest to get a family together whenever there are chores to be done.

26-15: A man's wrong doings can lead to his deserved undoings.

26-16: Goodness is far better than one's prettiness.

26-17: Ordinary men will have the will but, extraordinary men will find the way.

26-18: The weaker member of a successful partnership is usually smart enough to keep things as they are.

26-19: When hungry sharks follow a ship's stern, sailors are asked to forego a swim.

26-20: To see a stack of hay along the highway, it means good fortune for the day.

26-21: Encountering a herd of animals on the road tells you to slow down and stop.

26-22: Every time someone walks on the turf where you are to be buried, you should feel the shivers.

26-23: A shoestring that is untied means that someone just spoke your name.

20-24: It is bad luck to walk with one shoe off.

26-25: New shoes will squeak until after they are paid for in full.

26-26: Don't let old shoes remain stationary. Attach them to anything that moves.

26-27: A pregnant mother who is about to give birth must not see a falling star or her child will be stillborn.

26-28: If you sing at the table during supper, you will urinate in your bed on that night.

26-29: It is considered good luck to sing while bathing but, not if you bathe before breakfast.

26-30: Busy people are poor sleepers.

26-31: No man can live properly or die correctly unless he is married.

26-32: A smart wife knows her husband's faults better than he does.

26-33: A smarter wife ignores her husband's faults.

26-34: I never met a man that I liked until after we worked together.

26-35: Real men find excuses only for other people.

26-36: Real men have dignity.

26-37: Real men act as they believe.

26-38: The vanishing American is not the Indian. It's the honest American.

26-39: Honesty is one beginning that works well until the end.

26-40: All men may be born equal and all men may be granted equal rights under the law. However, the most important thing is this . . . . Which men have become equal to what? Ask the colored people if they have fully attained their lawful rights?

26-41: If you are sleepy after washing the dishes, company is coming.

26-42: After God created the Universe, he created man but, he was exhausted at the time.

26-43: Writing is one addiction that can improve the addicted.

26-44: There is nothing new that is completely new.

26-45: The best way to handle your credit rating is to be in a position where you don't need credit.

26-46: Bankers invented credit as a unique form of slavery.

26-47: Buying on credit will always cost more in the end.

26-48: A hammer keeps it head.

26-49: A hammer doesn't fly off at the handle.

26-50: A hammer will keep pounding away

Praise all Nations and all religions because there is ample room for each of us.

CHAPTER TWENTY-SEVEN
ITEMS 1-50

27-1: A hammer will find its mark.

27-2: A hammer drives the point home.

27-3: A hammer can clinch or save the point.

27-4: A hammer has more than one side.

27-5: A hammer that makes a mistake can start anew.

27-6: A hammer is one knocker that does well.

27-7: Be a good hammer.

27-8: A friend is someone whom you can borrow from and lend to.

27-9: Credibility should be your greatest goal.

27-10: Believe nothing that is written and less of what is spoken.

27-11: Honest people seem to be the most gullible persons.

27-12: Smoking will stunt your growth.

27-13: A petticoat that's showing means that your father loves you the most.

27-14: If you put on underwear with the wrong side out, don't change it. Wear it as it is or you will have bad luck.

27-15: Whiskey will rot your guts.

27-16: Bad women will be the ruination of young bachelors.

27-17: Dirty old men like virgins best.

27-18: Where there is one snake, there is always another.

27-19: Snap your fingers for good luck.

27-20: When you sneeze three times in succession, it's a sign of good luck.

27-21: If an adult sneezes, you should say, "Good Health". If a baby sneezes, you should ask, "Where are the wipes?"

27-22: Women get to make the soap but men have to stir the pot.

27-23: Women get to make the ice cream recipe but men get to stir the pot.

27-24: If you drop the soap, you may experience a misfortunate event in the Navy or in a prison.

27-25: What one has or what one is should never be controlling. What matters most is what one does.

27-26: Nothing is impossible unless you have to do it without help from anyone.

27-27: Every able-bodied man needs three things to succeed, a family, a home and a job.

27-28: A man becomes old after his parents are dead.

27-29: You know that you are old when your children are on Medicare.

27-30: Best leaders learn more from children.

27-31: First, you grow up and, second, you grow out.

27-32: Poverty and hunger are things that you leave behind after you start your College education or when you start your first meaningful job.

27-33: It is wise to always become better.

27-34: Don't judge appearances. Instead, judge accomplishments.

27-35: Marriage is a fine institution if, you are prepared for being institutionalized.

27-36: Happily married people are best known for their achievements, not their petty bedroom squabbles.

27-37: A well married man loves only his wife and family.

27-38: The marriage contract demands much from both bride and groom but, they both need to try and honor those commitments.

27-39: The greatest challenge to a young marriage is to learn how to sleep with someone else in the bed.

27-40: No new marriage can succeed without the learning of togetherness.

27-41: Marry the woman you love and love the woman you marry.

27-42: It is far more important to understand your husband than to understand his work.

27-43: Marriage is not concerned so much with finding the right person. More important is being the right person for him or her.

27-44: In your marriage, forget the word 'mine' but, always remember the word 'ours'.

27-45: Young people need to save something for their old age besides money. Instead, they need to save their marriage for themselves.

27-46: If you have a good wife, be thankful because many men don't.

27-47: If you have a bad wife, become a traveling salesman and sign her up for adult counseling.

27-48: Men manipulate mothers much better than wives do.

27-49: Once, I asked for a Janitor's job but, I was told that everyone in that Company had to have a college degree. This situation left me with a question and an answer. My answer was that I immediately enrolled at the University to pursue an engineering degree. My question was one of great sadness; namely, what hope can the uneducated people have if this trend continues?

27-50: Marriages don't fail, people fail.

Blessed are our leaders for they shall rule this Country for a minimum of four years. And, when they have done nothing but lie, cheat and steal, why don't we vote them out of office?

CHAPTER TWENTY-EIGHT
ITEMS 1-50

28-1: Marrying a woman for her beauty is like buying a car because of the paint job.

28-2: An ideal marriage has two key constituents, she and he.

28-3: To get what one expects, one must respect what one gets.

28-4: Speak when you are wrong but, be quiet when you are right.

28-5: The oldest profession is not whoring, it is parenthood.

28-6: Parents are people that bear children but, bore others with pictures of their kids.

28-7: Descendants are more interesting than ancestors because descendants can be improved.

28-8: Parents need to correct their own faults before correcting the faults of others.

28-9: Before marriage, we had strong thoughts about how kids ought to be reared. After marriage, we just had kids to try and keep up with.

28-10: I used to be a lot older than my kids but, now, they seem to be catching up with me.

28-11: Why do you put kids to bed early? To let them rest or to try and let yourself recover from your rigors of the day?

28-12: It is nice to watch your kids grow old and to realize that you no longer have to know everything.

28-13: My own children call me 'Papa'. My Grandchildren call me 'Papaw'. My great-grand-children call me 'Pap'. Now, they all need to call me their 'pauper'.

28-14: The perfect child for a typical male is a female.

28-15: Typically, children that are straight had straight parents.

28-16: Help a child and let the mother have some rest.

28-17: To be too busy for your children is to be too lonely later on.

28-18: The mother's manner is the child's best teacher.

28-19: Good mothers will have new shoes only after their children get new shoes.

28-20: Reading the Bible converts more people than preaching does.

28-21: The life of a working girl begins with her first born child.

28-22: Mothers are always hindered by the fact that there is never enough.

28-23: The mother that knows best is smart enough to say yes even if she has a headache.

28-24: A mother will always be noticed whenever she tries to steal a few moments of rest.

28-25: To discover a Robin's nest that contains eggs is a lucky event.

28-26: Never brush someone's hair when you are angry.

28-27: Burn bees to ashes and sprinkle those ashes on your feet to cure flat feet.

28-29: A circle protects against danger, especially in an Indian attack.

28-30: First fish caught must be returned to the water and that is a customary practice if you want to catch more fish.

28-31: Cats must never be allowed around sleeping children.

28-32: Hair continues to grow after death.

28-33: Women cannot keep secrets.

28-34: Tie a knot to keep a thought.

28-35: Beauty and brains rarely co-exist together in one person.

28-36: Babies born to older parents will be smarter.

28-37: If you cannot afford to buy the meat, hunt. If you can afford to buy the meat, don't hunt.

28-38: Snakes ward off disease.

28-39: Blondes may have more fun but, that's because they are the dumbest.

28-40: A woman's real education begins with her marriage.

28-41: Have a strong back and a weak mind which beats having a weak back and a strong mind.

28-42: Make vows on the Bible but, never on the Moon.

28-43: One good day redeems many bad ones.

28-44: To be happy, you must first want happiness.

28-45: Meanness is a curable disease.

28-46: Kindness given is more rewarding than kindness received.

28-47: Deny only yourself but, give freely to others.

28-48: Those who are not looking for success are the most likely candidates to find failure.

28-49: Give as much as you can.

28-50: Give until it hurts.

Be not silent if your enemies speak deceitful and use bad words against you.

CHAPTER TWENTY-NINE
ITEMS 1-50

29-1: Take less than you need.

29-2: Think about others more than yourself and you will discover happiness.

29-3: Those who give will have more and those who do not give will receive less.

29-4: Two can live as cheap as one if they really try.

29-5: I wish for you all of the success that you can handle.

29-6: We need to produce more happiness than we consume.

29-7: No one has ever been hurt by giving too much.

29-8: Place a high value upon yourself. Then, prove that you are worth it.

29-9: Slavery is defined by being unable to control one's own fate.

29-10: A long trip begins with that first step.

29-11: The primary mission of education is to develop character.

29-12: The purpose of an engineering education is to learn logic.

29-13: Imagination is the mother of invention.

29-14: Always want more than you have.

29-15: Medical science now admits that a new malignancy now exists, the decay of moral standards.

29-16: Love is the lubricant that lowers friction.

29-17: The wisest of men will not allow themselves to become angry.

29-18: Sometimes, we mind our children too much.

29-19: Before wisdom can arrive, knowledge must first pay a visit.

29-20: If we value comfort more than freedom, we could lose both.

29-21: Knowledge has no substitute.

29-22: The better way is always undiscovered.

29-23: Smart people discuss ideas while ordinary people discuss other things.

29-24: Small minds think about undermining others.

29-25: When the profit shrinks, the shrinks profit.

29-26: 'I do' is more important than 'IQ'.

29-27: Our character is best evaluated by our workmanship.

29-28: Talk about old things but keep an open mind about new ideas.

29-29: A bad example can sometimes radiate the best advice.

29-30: Today's greatest problems are not scientific, they are moral.

29-31: Knowledge is the goal for getting a college education, proving your manhood is not.

29-32: Invest in higher education because it offers the best payoff.

29-33: Want something too much and you are apt to get more than you wanted.

29-34: Breast feed a baby for a long time if you want to avoid getting pregnant too soon.

29-35: Breast feed a baby too long and you will have enormous tits.

29-36: Spinach will make you strong.

29-37: Heavy drinkers will have dumb kids.

29-38: Old dogs cannot learn new tricks.

29-39: Carry an acorn with you for good luck.

29-40: Adam and Eve were reincarnated as bald eagles.

29-41: The fox that flies is not a fox.

29-42: Never eat peanut skins.

29-43: Green crabapples make the stomach ache.

29-44: Wisdom knows what to do. Skill knows how to do it. But, virtue is just doing it.

29-45: Following the path of least resistance makes meandering rivers and crooked people.

29-46: Character is either won or awarded but, never given.

29-47: Society must never give a man his daily bread. Instead, Society should give man the opportunity to earn his daily bread.

29-48: Spend your vacation inside of your income, not outside of it.

29-49: What you will be, you are now becoming.

29-50: Anger has always corroded more than acid ever has.

Send a boy off to a war and he will return home as a man. Send a grown man off to war and, he probably will never return.

CHAPTER THIRTY
ITEMS 1-50

30-1: The solution to difficult problems lies within our capabilities.

30-2: Imagine that the entire election depends upon your vote and voting will become more meaningful.

30-3: Only educated people can entertain relevant thoughts about other people, places and necessary things. Here, the assumption is that our Congressmen and Congresswomen are educated.

30-4: Saints were sinners who tried harder.

30-5: Yesterday is a memory but, tomorrow is a mystery.

30-6: It's hard to learn if you are too busy talking.

30-7: Get wrapped-up in yourself because no one else will.

30-8: If you must become a package, be a useful one.

30-9: Blue flowers mean fidelity.

30-10: In baseball, never step on the foul lines. That brings bad luck.

30-11: Beaver fat is good for burns.

30-12: Tie a white ribbon to a beehive if a wedding is planned.

30-13: Get off on the right foot for success.

30-14: Cast pennies into the water well or fountains for good luck.

30-15: Birth control is a sin that fights off creation.

30-16: Birth marks usually mean that a bad experience occurred during a given pregnancy.

30-17: Never remove your wedding ring until the wedding ceremony is over.

30-18: Legalized gambling includes your marriage, it can be a roll of the dice.

30-19: A husband with a great imagination has a satisfied wife.

30-20: People who come apart at the seams were never properly joined.

30-21: For marriage to work best, both man and wife need to work harder.

30-22: If you are pushing 85-years of age, watch how you push.

30-23: Memories cost you a part of your life.

30-24: Young people rarely use their youth wisely.

30-25: Pimples are caused by bad blood.

30-26: Blue blood is the sign of nobility.

30-27: Kiss a new baby on the forehead for good luck.

30-28: The appearance of a blue-ish or green-ish moon means a good fortune.

30-29: Too much bread will cause obesity.

30-30: Pray for a good crop but, never stop hoeing.

30-31: If something accidentally passes between two persons that are walking, say 'bread and butter' quickly or both persons will face bad luck.

30-32: Forty is old to the young but, sixty is still young to the old.

30-33: The future of our Nation depends upon the education of our children.

30-34: A college education produces little harm if you are willing to start learning more after your graduation day.

30-35: The best gift of all is to give something of your own to one that is more deserving.

30-36: A college class is defined as ignorance in action.

30-37: Don't talk about yourself at a party. Leave early and let the others address that challenge.

30-38: A friend will see you through to the finish but, all others will try to see that you are finished.

30-39: If you are asked to give testimony about cheating, don't cheat.

30-40: Our body's best wealth lies mainly within our minds.

30-41: Turning off someone's light doesn't address the darkness.

30-42: If everybody tried to do about one-half of what we expect them to do, all things would be vastly improved.

30-43: One's life should be lived so that it will be long remembered.

30-44: We can split the atom but we can't unite the people.

30-45: Those who do little things well can be trusted to do big things better.

30-46: Those that know everything have stopped thinking.

30-47: Democracy requires a lot but, delivers more.

30-48: Work shoes make a better impression than sneakers do.

30-49: It wasn't raining when Noah started building the Arc.

30-50: If everybody in America gave China a single 100-dollar bill, our debt would be more than fulfilled.

If you are looking for help or guidance, look within your own mind.
Don't look elsewhere.

CHAPTER THIRTY-ONE
ITEMS 1-50

31-1: What is expensive we revere much too highly.

31-2: Obligations and problems surround each of us.

31-3: Wisdom is expensive because the demand always exceeds the supply.

31-4: The day was wasted if nothing of value was done.

31-5: Progress is the sum of small deeds done by many good people.

31-6: Some people have too much weakness and too little will power.

31-7: The first to kiss the bride should be her father.

31-8: Thrice a bridesmaid but, never a bride.

31-9: Unlucky at cards but, lucky in love.

31-10: Never chew on a broom straw. It brings bad luck.

31-11: Brunettes are more sincere.

31-12: Some blondes are smart in the things that really matter, mine was.

31-13: If bubbles collect at the center of your coffee cup, you will inherit some money.

31-14: Albinos are not a freak of nature and they should be respected.

31-15: A deer's tooth will bring good luck.

31-16: Camphor cures a cold in the chest.

31-17: Canaries bring harmony to the home.

31-18: Ripe cranberries will help with skin cancer.

31-19: Baking soda is the best tooth powder.

31-20: Porcupines throw their quills when threatened.

31-21: When squirrels are scarce in autumn, it will be a long winter.

31-22: When your back is up against the wall, put your best shoulder into it.

31-23: Keep your nose close to the grinding wheel.

31-24: Creative thought is wisdom that is gleaned from knowledge.

31-25: In this life, you must know the difference between a mule and a jackass. One works hard while the other always kicks.

31-26: Try to look like a thoroughbred even if you have behaved like a jackass.

31-27: Small deeds finished are better than large deeds unfinished.

31-28: You can't be hurt too much by the things that you didn't say.

31-29: Inactivity is both irksome and boring.

31-30: The heaviest stress to bear is a chip on your shoulder.

31-31: The best way to evaluate thought is to do something.

31-32: The people that are too dumb to be honest are your crooks and thieves.

31-33: Give someone a piece of your mind and you lose more than you gain.

31-34: You don't have to retract words that you didn't use.

31-35: John Wayne never recanted on any issue, absolutely none.

31-36: These days, charity is a business.

31-37: Education controls the young and gives solace to the aged.

31-38: Leftovers can be poisonous if they grow their own coat.

31-39: To change your luck, turn the back of your chair toward the table and sit astride the chair. Men like to see a woman in control of things.

31-40: Oysters make a good poultice for a black eye.

31-41: Throwing unwanted kittens in the river will bring on bad weather.

31-42: If a cat is thrown into the air, that cat will always land on his feet.

31-43: For best chances of survival, have your babies in the Spring.

31-44: It is bad luck to break the sequence of a chain letter.

31-45: Too many people behave like chameleons.

31-46: When four businessmen meet and shake hands in a cross-wise manner, one of the four businessmen will fail.

31-47: Geniuses and criminals are more easily frustrated.

31-48: A sneeze expels part of your spirit forever.

31-49: A double chin marks a glutton.

31-50: No one is useless who helps another.

There is great power and unity within a small family. Let no other man try to set them apart.

CHAPTER THIRTY-TWO
ITEMS 1-50

32-1: Tea doesn't cause intoxication.

32-2: Chestnuts are a symbol of longevity and fertility.

32-3: Butternuts are a symbol of everlasting friendship.

32-4: Canaries are good gas detectors inside of coal mines.

32-5: No one should falter at the altar.

32-6: Looking forward to your career is nice but, looking backward at all your achievements is a lot more enjoyable.

32-7: The airplane takes off into the wind as your career does.

32-8: To thy own self, be true.

32-9: Gossip and news are almost identical except that news is heard and gossip is told.

32-10: Let your light shine.

32-11: To make ends meet, you have to get off your own rear end.

32-12: The greatest guilt is to say that you have no guilt.

32-13: A self-taught society has a limited knowledge.

32-14: There is no wrong way of doing right just as there is no right way of doing wrong.

32-15: A temptation is not always a good opportunity.

32-16: Treat your enemies as you would treat your friends.

32-17: Businessmen are gamblers. They provide services for profit but at a known risk.

32-18: It is better to have one good idea than several bad ones.

32-19: The greatest distance that we can travel always begins within us.

32-20: Touch wood and remember the cross of Jesus.

32-21: In sports, the team that sheds first blood usually loses.

32-22: Once each year is enough for the Christmas season.

32-23: Elves and fairies work to protect morals from doing harm.

32-24: Crows are harbingers of misfortune.

32-25: Blow cigarette smoke into the ears for ear ache relief.

32-26: Pregnant women should never attend funeral wakes.

32-27: The larger the diamond, the greater the misfortune.

32-28: Bread dough must be beaten in a clockwise manner.

32-29: Stones taken from a fish are symbols of good luck.

32-30: Cod liver oil is good for rheumatism.

32-31: Carry a coin with a hole in it and you will be lucky.

32-32: Wear a dirty stocking around your throat to cure a sore throat.

32-33: Using a dead man's comb will make you bald.

32-34: Alcoholism is inherited.

32-35: Kids liking alcoholic drinks is usually a problem created by their grandparents.

32-36: Blow the foam off of your beer mug for good luck.

32-37: A drunk will never tell a white lie, that kind of liar will always tell bold ones.

32-38: A chip on the shoulder means that a stone sits higher up.

32-39: Men are neither good nor bad. We share different amounts of both in all of us.

32-40: Does right make might or does might make right?

32-41: When you assault another person, the long term regret or pain is for yourself.

32-42: Live like a good person and die with poise.

32-43: Opportunities make us what we are.

32-44: If something has been done just one way for a long time, it usually means that improvement is badly needed.

32-45: You can't reach Heaven without some knowledge of the jungle.

32-46: It is more rewarding to do honest labor and to give services that are needed.

32-47: Success should not be inherited, it needs to be earned.

32-48: Wealth means more if it is accumulated by yourself.

32-49: Hard work strengthens character.

32-50: One experience teaches more than a thousand warnings.

Water will cover your adversaries just as it did for Moses and his people.

CHAPTER THIRTY-THREE
ITEMS 1-50

33-1: Most people have interests but, only a few have firm beliefs.

33-2: The World's richest man can be an honest one but, don't count on it.

33-3: Money can't buy more sunrises for anyone.

33-4: Sunsets are gifted items and they aren't for sale.

33-5: Those that yell the most about equality are, generally, the most inferior.

33-6: A shortage never guarantees success yet, it does help to drive the price upwards.

33-7: Strangers are unknown friends.

33-8: Happiness lies someplace between too little and too much.

33-9: Every person knows more than you about some things.

33-10: Stars twinkle if they like what they are seeing.

33-11: Memorial Day is held in honor of all fallen heroes, particularly those that were killed by friendly fire.

33-12: Unmarried women should not attend cornerstone ceremonies.

33-13: Swans always sing before they die. Why can't we be equally fearless?

33-14: Goose grease will cure cramps.

33-15: She's as blind as a bat but, she will be the first to find a coin that is dropped on the floor.

33-16: Cows give more milk if music is played for them during the milking session.

33-17: The cow that delivers Hershey's chocolate candy bars is in a great demand.

33-18: If you want blue skin, marry your kin.

33-19: It is bad luck to place your hat on the top of your bed.

33-20: Turn your baseball cap backwards for good luck.

33-21: Evil spirits prefer women with long hair.

33-22: If your hair crackles, evil spirits are talking to you.

33-23: Turbans are worn to keep Middle East vermin from spreading.

33-24: Partly cloudy is interpreted by others as being partly sunny.

33-25: A cup that is unfilled needs filling.

33-26: It is easy to follow someone who has left so many stones upturned.

33-27: One who asks, "What's the use" will never grasp the opportunity.

33-28: Happiness, peace and prosperity are common goals.

33-29: Know the price well but, know the value better.

33-30: Friendship is the cement that binds people together.

33-31: People can be judged by the size of their eraser or by the length of their wooden pencil.

33-32: Teachers without any short pieces of chalk cannot be good teachers.

33-33: Talented people avoid work by doing it right the first time.

33-34: White lung disease from too much chalk dust is a common problem among the best and oldest Professors.

33-35: Most of us know how to be quiet but very few of us know when to start being quiet.

33-36: Be better to others but be best to yourself.

33-37: Ulcers are caused by making too much of too little for too long.

33-38: Downtrodden people do nothing, say nothing and remain nothing.

33-39: As you get closer to home during your commute, put a 'smiley face' on.

33-40: As you get closer to home, install your gentler mood.

33-41: Hold thread between your teeth while you are sewing.

33-42: Rock the cradle with your left foot.

33-43: The greatest athletes die young.

33-44: One man's meal is another man's feast.

33-45: Never kill a cricket on a Sunday.

33-46: Stumbling is an evil omen. Try to be more careful.

33-47: Wear earrings to cure blood-shot eyes.

33-48: Never touch a blind man's clothing.

33-49: In face of danger, make a sign of the cross.

33-50: Keep your legs crossed to avoid becoming pregnant.

Make known your deeds as someone is always in need of knowing them.

CHAPTER THIRTY-FOUR
ITEMS 1-50

34-1: Keep your legs crossed for good luck.

34-2: Cross-stitch embroidery will protect the home from harm.

34-3: As cock-eyed as an owl is like being as cock-eyed as a drunk.

34-4: As crazy as a horse.

34-5: As stubborn as a mule.

34-6: As silly as a jackass.

34-7: Crystal gazing is for simple minds.

34-8: Gazing balls are for children to break and for old men to replace.

34-9: Too much is published about staying young and too little is said about growing old.

34-10: It is better to suffer wrong than to do wrong.

34-11: Never cheated means that you have never trusted anyone.

34-12: Ignorant people are never free to make their own government.

34-13: Be like the mirror and always reflect the truth.

34-14: Small airplanes must watch the weather and stay close to home. Large airplanes can go most anywhere they want so be a large airplane.

34-15: It is nice to be wealthy but it's more important to be healthy.

34-16: Pay your debts if you want to be respected.

34-17: Conceit is widespread among smaller people.

34-18: Becoming civil is the first step toward being kind.

34-19: When you leave a bad situation, don't leave a forwarding address.

34-20: One who is afraid will always make trouble.

34-21: If you hear a cuckoo brother of mine brag in the morning, it usually means that some woman was hurt during the night.

34-22: A cuckoo person is one that is eccentric or unconventional as all my brothers are.

34-23: When the whippoorwill calls, someone dear will die.

34-24: A daddy-long-legs spider is supposed to bring good luck to the onlooker.

34-25: Dead bodies should never be carried aboard ocean-going vessels, only ashes are acceptable.

34-26: Goats will eat damned near anything, even tin cans.

34-27: Left-handed people hear better on their left side.

34-28: Ear wax must be removed if you want to hear things better.

34-29: Ears must be washed if they are to remain healthy.

34-30: If a woman wants to be kissed by her beau, she must wear his hat.

34-31: Death is contagious to all but, you only have it once, never twice.

34-32: Flat-chested women seem to have less sickness.

34-33: Turkeys prefer a dry bath in the dust.

34-34: People with diabetes need to bathe in saltwater.

34-35: Sauerkraut juice cures diabetes.

34-36: Alfalfa tea is good for the diabetic.

34-37: Diamonds don't wear out but, they have to be cleaned on a regular basis.

34-38: Rub dice on a red-haired person for good luck.

34-39: Fat people are overfed and lazy.

34-40: Thin people are underfed but always active.

34-41: It is beautiful to learn but divine to be tolerant.

34-42: The learning process provides a new life.

34-43: We are the sum total of our experience.

34-44: What is learned must be passed on to others.

34-45: Education brings people together.

34-46: Collective judgments are usually wrong.

34-47: We all come from somewhere and we each fear where we are headed.

34-48: A pang of confidence can be a serious pain.

34-49: I miss my hometown almost as much as I miss my childhood.

34-50: Bear your own existence.

Scouts are always prepared and good Scouts make great leaders.

CHAPTER THIRTY-FIVE
ITEMS 1-50

35-1: There is no love without some agreement and there can be no agreements without some love.

35-2: Never want your past to become someone's future.

35-3: The most important lesson to learn in college is how to take a test.

35-4: Some men wonder what might have been rather than what is.

35-5: Too much gin makes boys of men.

35-6: If you've seen Heaven on Earth, then you must have had a happy family.

35-7: Scared people are the ones to fear the most.

35-8: Encourage your brothers to live their own life well. Don't try to live it for them.

35-9: Hide fright and show courage.

35-10: Don't run from anything that is chasing you.

35-11: If you are afraid of one thing, most other things are also frightening.

35-12: Blessed are men that go around in circles because they shall be called 'Big Wheels'.

35-13: The humblest of citizens are those that pursue a righteous cause.

35-14: Pennies saved for a rainy day won't buy much of an umbrella, not at today's prices.

35-15: Treat compliments too lightly and the giver might stop giving them.

35-16: Bills and colds are much too abundant.

35-17: God, help us because we have become like the French people.

35-18: TV is a poor substitute for a good book.

35-19: I like to write books but, I like selling them better.

35-20: Won't some patron of the arts please sponsor me?

35-21: Be an honest person so that the World will have one less rascal.

35-22: Faith is intelligence in action.

35-23: By the time that most men become successful, they are too old to enjoy it properly.

35-24: Enjoy the struggle but savor the success.

35-25: A brave man respects strength without being afraid of it.

35-26: If anybody steals your thunder, make more thunder.

35-27: One of the hardest things to learn is that truth is more important than consequence.

35-28: A dimple in your cheeks and many hearts you will seek.

35-29: A dimple in your chin and many hearts you will win.

35-30: Eat the flesh of a dog and become a Mexican peon.

35-31: The cooing of a dove is a sign of bad news.

35-32: A hope chest is the bride's best dowry.

35-33: A son should not marry until after all of the daughters have been wed.

35-34: A ringing in the ear is the worst bell of all because only one person can hear it.

35-35: Night air is considered to be evil air.

35-36: Drafts of hot or cold air are movements made by spirits, both good and bad.

35-37: When you take a picture of someone, you trap their soul.

35-38: We act as we think and some of us act as we stink.

35-39: We dream what we want to be and not all dreams come true.

35-40: We pray for what we want or need and not all prayers are answered.

35-41: We are as we are, not what others want us to be.

35-42: Women drown face downward but, men drown face upward.

35-43: From the viewpoint of the sheep, shepherds and wool gatherers are as parasitic as lice.

35-44: A child who has known only comforts shall expect only comforts.

35-45: A good mother will not accept treats until after her children have been given treats.

35-46: Life is a constant struggle until the final struggle.

35-47: The wonder of desert sand is that each grain is different.

35-48: Do explorers really want to find something ahead or is it that they earnestly want to leave something behind. Here, my thoughts are about Columbus and Isabella.

35-49: See a Kentucky Cardinal in the morning and feel no hunger that night.

35-50: No one asks to be born.

Wandering from Nation to Nation and job to job is no way to live. Ask the Gypsies.

CHAPTER THIRTY-SIX
ITEMS 1-50

36-1: A ride in a horse-drawn carriage can be very romantic until the horse expels gas.

36-2: Keeping a house up can wear a good man down.

36-3: The tax assessor is appreciated only by his mother.

36-4: Greed traps more criminals than fingerprints do.

36-5: Song of my heart and rhythm of my being, don't fail me just yet because there is still too much that is undone and not yet ready.

36-6: If you must write, write as much as you can.

36-7: When I was little, things were too large and, now that I am large, things are too little.

36-8: The only logical part of a newspaper these days is the sports page.

36-9: Common sense prevents good sense from becoming nonsense.

36-10: At one time, oranges were known as round candy balls and a gift from God.

36-11: Texas has two seasons, January-through-March and summer.

36-12: The most inexcusable form of wrongful death involved frozen blue ice from airplane toilets.

36-13: If women are now allowed to sit in the cock-pit, shouldn't we call it a cunt-pit?

36-14: I am most frightened by some of the spirits that come from a distillery.

36-15: One that gave his life to metals will never receive any medals.

36-16: Keeping a house too clean drives the woman mad or mean.

36-17: While some of the sick pray for a quick death, others that are dying, pray for a longer life.

36-18: The white berries of mistletoe come from Heaven.

36-19: The pheasant drums a good tune but makes a better meal.

36-20: When you cannot think, whistle. And, when you cannot whistle, think.

36-21: The Bald Eagle brought fire from Heaven and gave it to man.

36-22: Nibbling caraway seeds will enhance the hearing.

36-23: Most of our problems are caused by what we eat.

36-24: Birds and horses eat all of the time but, do we have to follow their bad example?

36-25: Stay indoors during an eclipse.

36-26: Moon tides are maddening.

36-27: Benedict Arnold should be burned in effigy on every 4th of July.

36-28: Never bring bird eggs inside of the house. That brings bad luck.

36-29: It is unlucky to harvest the henhouse after dark.

36-30: Eat fish on Fridays as the Catholics do.

36-31: Sexual diseases are sins of the flesh.

36-32: Elephants remember well.

36-33: When you ride a motorcycle, keep your mouth closed.

36-34: Trouble is like a big curve in the road. Both are straightened out after they are properly approached.

36-35: The best test for indispensability is to place your fingers in a bucket full of water. Slowly withdraw your fingers from the water and for a determination of any effects which you might have exerted on the aqueous system.

36-36: Don't bad mouth people behind their back. Instead, say what you have to say to their face.

36-37: What money cannot buy are the real treasures.

36-38: One who rests upon his reputation sleeps on the wrong side of the bed.

36-39: Don't be down on something that you aren't up on.

36-40: When some try to imitate strength, others might declare it to be rudeness.

36-41: Buying on the cuff may cause you to lose your shirt.

36-42: It is nice to be able to speak in different languages. However, keeping your mouth closed is absolutely priceless.

36-43: Happiness is not pleasure but, it is close.

36-44: Success demands the line of greatest persistence.

36-45: If you become well qualified, you won't be without work for very long.

36-46: Workers of today school their way through work. In my day, one worked his way through school.

36-47: Worry and rocking chairs have much in common. Both will keep you occupied but, neither one of these two will get you anywhere.

36-48: Believe in yourself but, be hard to convince.

36-49: Bad kids are like airplane crashes in that both get a lot of publicity.

36-50: The best liar is the one with the best memory.

Remember the wonderful works of the World's greatest engineer and become like him, if you can.

CHAPTER THIRTY-SEVEN
ITEMS 1-50

37-1: Before you can wear his crown in Heaven, you must first bear his cross on Earth.

37-2: If you have to cry over spilled milk, try to condense the crying.

37-3: First place may not be all that it is cracked up to be but, it sure beats second place.

37-4: Do what you must where you are with whatever you have for whomever you can and don't ask why.

37-5: If life is too empty, just 'fill-her-up'.

37-6: Sailors are well guided by stars over the oceans and badly influenced by all Hollywood starlets.

37-7: If you can't do great things well, then do small things better.

37-8: Don't be an atheist, be something more meaningful.

37-9: Snakes are always given the right-of-way.

37-10: Old timers know that 'on time' means something which involves punctuality. Youngsters of today view 'on time' as the final date to ask for deferred payments.

37-11: Every human race began as a mongrel race.

37-12: Have a lucky hand and fill the cooking pot.

37-13: The strongest ones have more fits and more strokes.

37-14: Never carry your rifle over your left shoulder.

37-15: Finding a sea shell near your front door will cause good luck to enter your house.

37-16: Male babies are created on the right side but female babies are created on the left side.

37-17: Boy babies are carried lower in the womb than girl babies.

37-18: Loose eyelashes must be destroyed.

37-19: Women must pluck their eyebrows after they get married.

37-20: A mother-in-law will always bring bad news.

37-21: Being a second wife is always harder than being a first wife.

37-22: One marriage should be enough if properly managed.

37-23: If a married man looks for something better, he is apt to find more of the same, with different appearances.

37-24: All women use the toilet in the same manner as men, don't lust for them.

37-25: A protruding chin means great strength.

37-26: Lips betray the character.

37-27: A large mouth denotes generosity.

37-28: If you fall uphill, you are one lucky person.

37-29: Wear socks with white toes to avoid falling.

37-30: Always walk with your longest leg downhill.

37-31: Always climb a mountain from the East to the West.

37-32: When you climb one mountain, look forward to the next one.

37-33: Mountain men look down on flatlanders.

37-34: Citizens of the valley want to live higher-up.

37-35: Only mountain people can have a natural 'high' from the air that we breathe.

37-36: Hill country is the best country.

37-37: If you live on a mountain top, you live closer to God.

37-38: Mountains don't change but Mountaineers do.

37-39: Mountain men make better husbands.

37-40: The trees on the mountains make clean air for me to breathe. Why trade all that for the filthy exhaust pipes of the big city?

37-41: There are two sources of known intelligence, the heart and the brain.

37-42: No man can help another person without also helping himself.

37-43: The pursuit of freedom and equality must never end.

37-44: I find it difficult to get by on the salary that I always dreamed of getting.

37-45: He that thinks about the inch but, talks by the yard needs to be given the foot.

37-46: Sweet attracts more attention than sour does.

37-47: Forming opinions without getting the facts may save time and money but, it can cause loss of life through failure.

37-48: He that likes himself too much has very few friends.

37-49: If you have a one-man business to operate, your greatest concern should be the bad boss or the lazy employee.

37-50: There is a very thin line between being tired and being lazy.

Be merciful and kind to all of your employees and reap the harvest of success.

CHAPTER THIRTY-EIGHT
ITEMS 1-50

38-1: Stand up for your rights but, follow through on your duties.

38-2: The best test for any College Department is measured by how their graduates perform after graduation is over.

38-3: Justice makes democracy attractive but, injustice makes democracy mandatory.

38-4: One writer's imagination is another man's fantasy.

38-5: One man's creation is another man's envy.

38-6: Where big words fail, smaller ones often succeed.

38-7: Small ideas and big ideas can't be compared to one great idea,

38-8: Never let too much of yesterday take too much of today.

38-9: Make friends before you need them.

38-10: Leadership looks easy if someone else does it.

38-11: There are people who make things happen and there are people who watch things happen but, the problem is that we have too many people who never know when something important has happened.

38-12: There are people who lead and there are people that follow but, unfortunately, there are too many others that aren't going anywhere soon.

38-13: A weak person is defined as one who remains silent when he ought to speak or one that speaks when he ought to stay silent.

38-14: Strong, successful types know when to speak and when not to.

38-15: Anger and danger are different by just a single 'd'.

38-16: Give some people an inch and they will take a mile before behaving like a six-inch ruler.

38-17: To exist is a waste of time but, to live a full life, one needs to always use his time more wisely.

38-18: Overhaul of character begins with both you and I.

38-19: Story tellers have short fingernails.

38-20: A shooting star toward the right is good but, a shooting star to the left is bad.

38-21: He that lies will also blush if he was reared correctly.

38-22: When one dies on Earth, a family circle is broken. In Heaven, that circle will never be broken.

38-23: Plant a tree whenever a child is born.

38-24: When a child dies, a tree must be felled.

38-25: The woman who dreams of fish will soon become pregnant.

38-26: Always be aware of the dark and, moreover, seek the light.

38-27: When you sneeze, you have to admit that you kissed a stranger.

38-28: Sleep on the right side of your body for good luck.

38-29: Rub a dead tree trunk for good luck.

38-30: An hour of sleep before midnight is most beneficial.

38-31: The perfect twenty-four hour day is split into three parts, Eight hours for working, eight hours for playing and eight hours for sleeping.

38-32: When in bed, your head should face due North.

38-33: Fireflies are worms that fly.

38-34: A white spot on your thumbnail means that a good fortune will soon arrive.

38-35: The oldest child will always do more in life than the youngest child.

38-36: Fish should be eaten to feed the brain.

38-37: Eat stale food and suffer dreams.

38-38: Eat too much food and lose sleep.

38-39: Eat contaminated food and stay on the toilet for hours.

38-40: Sweet clover will make the cow sick.

38-41: An honest father leaves his children much wealth but, very little money.

38-42: Tourists are people that spend their children's inheritance.

38-43: If everyone took care of their own mess, this World would be a cleaner place.

38-44: With a mind that is clear, everything around you will be clearer.

38-45: Throwing trash from a car window spoils the landscape and accomplishes very little.

38-46: Our Pentagon maintains that the best way to preserve peace is to always prepare for war.

38-47: One has to ignore what cannot be changed.

38-48: If you stand for something, you will fail for less.

38-49: Knowing something is a good beginning. What you learn afterwards is what really counts.

38-50: If you take insults well, expect more.

Fools, when will you become wise? Which one of us will go against the wicked?

CHAPTER THIRTY-NINE
ITEMS 1-50

39-1: Green tea will make you pee.

39-2: Half of the people don't know how the other half should live but both halves have strong opinions about the subject.

39-3: The greatest sin is not the doing of evil deeds. Instead, the greatest sin is allowing such deeds to be done.

39-4: Remember that total darkness does not exist and that there are 650,000 shades of gray.

39-5: The weaker the cause, the stronger the words.

39-6: The best curfew is to remove all parents off the streets by 2200-hours.

39-7: It is nice to have many thoughts about all of the issues but, it is a lot safer to live in a Country where you can practice your freedom of thought.

39-8: In the ladder of life, move to the highest rung that is available. Then, retreat by one rung for security reasons.

39-9: Opportunity favors those who are prepared.

39-10: My Country owes me nothing. I was given the same opportunity that every other boy and girl was given.

39-11: A reckless driver is one who passes your car in spite of all that you can do.

39-12: Ford drivers should be given the right-of-way on the highway but, there are some Chevrolet drivers who disagree with that principle.

39-13: Drunken drivers will stray where others stay.

39-14: The concept of 'don't drink and drive' does work.

39-15: One test of character comes when we are forced to park in a minority zone for the very first time.

39-16: Our future life is governed by the education that we seek.

39-17: You shouldn't do for others what they won't do for themselves.

39-18: He that stumbles without falling is wiser.

39-19: Flat-chested women complain about being cheated.

39-20: What's the big deal about flat-chested women? Eventually, all tits go flat anyway.

39-21: Frog legs are the delicacy of the river.

39-22: Blind ponies are the best ponies for working inside of the coal mines.

39-23: You don't have to be dumb to work in the coal mines but, it does help.

39-24: Digging coal is hard work but, somebody has to do it.

39-25: Black gold for one is black lung for another.

39-26: Never eat lobster and ice cream at the same meal.

39-27: Lettuce will make you sleep better.

39-28: Eating meat causes high blood pressure.

39-29: Strawberries will cause milk to curdle before its time.

39-30: Hard to chew foods strengthens the teeth.

39-31: Never eat too much or too often since that leads to stomach problems.

39-32: Dark bread is healthier than white bread.

39-33: Cucumbers keep a salad cool.

39-34: Bathe your feet daily.

39-35: Never place your shoes on a table or a bed. That brings bad luck.

39-36: A genius who is capable without being able defines frustration.

39-37: Don't ever believe that the lily is related to the onion.

39-38: Regarding movies, the ending is always more meaningful than the beginning.

39-39: Cut grass before it becomes hay.

39-40: Men that become rich quickly are never innocent.

39-41: Words without any action does far less than action without any words.

39-42: Our future depends on our long-range vision.

39-43: Quality means more than quantity does.

39-44: It is easier to become smart than it is to hide being dumb.

39-45: The habitual liar lives a tragic life because he cannot trust anyone.

39-46: Spoken words leave less doubt but, written words leave all doubt.

39-47: Too much use is called abuse.

39-48: When you bury the hatchet, don't build a monument.

39-49: Every rule for success involves work.

39-50: A man is what he is because of what he has been.

He who lives on top of the biggest mountain is best informed or the richest or both.

CHAPTER FORTY
ITEMS 1-50

40-1: Know where you want to be someday and try to make it happen.

40-2: A dropped hammer means that love is on the way.

40-3: The best good luck charm is the four-leaf clover.

40-4: A shrewd ill-tempered woman makes the best mate for some men but, not for me.

40-5: Fire caused by God's lightening cannot be extinguished using water.

40-6: Never throw cold water on the face of a sleeping person.

40-7: Witches have their meetings only on Fridays.

40-8: The one change to fear the most is called the change of life.

40-9: Plant by the Moon but, harvest under the Sun.

40-10: Keep black dogs away from the graveyard until after the burial has been completed.

40-11: The toughest part of the arts is called self-management.

40-12: The toughest part of the sciences is called ethics.

40-13: We don't need guided missiles unless we have misguided leaders.

40-14: Crime is not for the majority because the payback is much too high.

40-15: Crime doesn't pay because it is wrong.

40-16: Some people who don't get what they deserve ought to be more grateful.

40-17: What happened to Miami is happening to Houston, more Spanish-speaking people than we need or want.

40-18: Home invaders concentrate on the elderly or the sick.

40-19: If there is ever a city named 'failure', its government will be run by lawyers.

40-20: Be on the right tract but, never stay put. You might get run over by the maddening crowd.

40-21: Never work at a job long enough to do anything wrong.

40-22: Vacant lots are a lot like vacant minds, they collect too much trash.

40-23: Only those who have the patience to do simple things perfectly will ever acquire the skills to do harder things well.

40-24: Never oppose something because you don't understand. Some things are best if they remain misunderstood.

40-25: If you fall down many times, get up more often.

40-26: It requires more muscles to frown than it does to smile so be efficient, smile more often.

40-27: Look for a way to get something done. Don't waste time searching for excuses.

40-28: Experience is always helpful if something bad happens to you.

40-29: The harder you fall, the higher you bounce if you are made of the right stuff.

40-30: Voting is one way to make important changes.

40-31: Maturity gives us the ability to get over being hurt by someone.

40-32: Maturity is the ability to do one's assignments without being watched.

40-33: There are seven little helpers for the published author; namely, what, why, when, how, who, which and where.

40-34: Better lenses see more of that which was previously overlooked.

40-35: Everybody wants a four-day work-week but, nobody wants to give up their overtime pay.

40-36: Since it takes most people six days to finish their work assignments, the idea of a four-day work-week is beyond all reasonable logic. Don't hold your breath.

40-37: Education is a life-long trip. It is not a single destination trip.

40-38: Don't be so well-rounded that you can't move in a preferred direction.

40-39: Doing your best at this time may not be critical but, it is good practice for the time when critical will be mandated.

40-40: The worst invention ever was called an excuse.

40-41: Truth that is stretched too far will, one day, snap back at you.

40-42: Take life inch-by-inch because it too hard if taken yard-by-yard.

40-43: Satisfaction in life requires constructive accomplishments.

40-44: Ideas that fly need a place to land.

40-45: How can honesty ever be the best policy if we allow cheating to go unpunished?

40-46: What a tangled web we weave, when we first deceive.

40-47: A genius is an unbalanced person on the positive side.

40-48: Success depends more on what you give up to achieve whatever you take up.

40-49: Always carry a pair of loaded dice in your pocket and you will never be without some money.

40-50: Demons are allergic to the odor of garlic.

If enemies taunt, that is to be expected. If friends taunt, that is abnormal and totally unexpected.

CHAPTER FORTY-ONE
ITEMS 1-50

41-1: Stand in front of a full-length mirror and eat an apple on Halloween night. Before you can finish eating the apple, the face of your true love will be revealed by the mirror.

41-2: The only proper gift for a lady is candy or flowers. Give her anything that suggests work and that will prove to be disastrous for your relationship.

41-3: Place a goat horn under your pillow for insomnia.

41-4: Goldfish are a recommended gift for younger lovers.

41-5: If you hear the geese honk while high in the sky, something is wrong.

41-6: If your grandfather clock casts a shadow that resembles a coffin, death will soon enter that household.

41-7: Leave your grandfather clock running if you want to hear the 'ding-dongs' all night long.

41-8: To be 'on-the-square' means that you are an honest person.

41-9: A good pilot's greatest fear is still gremlins.

41-10: When sea gulls fly inland, rain is coming.

41-11: Some members of Parliament got to know Guy Fawkes pretty well but, not for very long. Then, Guy's bomb exploded which means that England started terrorism.

41-12: If a woman's hair turns gray on one side only, she will soon become a widow.

41-13: The baby that is born with a heavy down will be a good baby.

41-14: Cross your hands when crossing a creek.

41-15: If the first customer on a Friday morning is an elderly lady, next week's sales will be less than normal.

41-16: Never eat hare if you live near a cemetery.

41-17: Wear a triangular kerchief as a headdress for good luck.

41-18: The only good hawk is a dead one.

41-19: Steal hay on Christmas Eve and feed it to your cattle on Christmas Day if you want better cows.

41-20: Never eat eggs which appear more round than oval.

41-21: Exercise for the body and read for the mind.

41-22: Opportunity always seems more attractive after it has gone than before it arrived.

41-23: Know the hard way to do something but, find a way to do it easier.

41-24: Faith can move mountains.

41-25: If enthusiasm could be raised as easily as suspicion is raised, think of all the good that could be done.

41-26: Losing one's temper is not the best way to get rid of it.

41-27: Sin builds a huge mountain that only good faith can remove.

41-28: A grave may be enclosed to total darkness but, a grave is also a portal that can lead to everlasting light.

41-29: Trust people and they will be true to you.

41-30: Treat people great and all will become greater.

41-31: Today's motorist drives a mortgaged vehicle over a bond-financed highway using credit-card fuel.

41-32: The exercise programs that do the greatest harm to your mind are cited as follows: jumping to conclusions, running down your friends, side-stepping responsibilities, pushing your luck, rowing another man's boat and walking on somebody's grave.

41-33: Light all the fuses that you can but, stand clear for any explosions.

41-34: The best teacher develops the student's ability to fend for himself.

41-35: You cannot succeed by being who you are. Success comes to those who are what they are.

41-36: Some success comes from knowledge but, most of it comes from doing something worthwhile.

41-37: Serendipity is not destiny. It's more like luck than anything else.

41-38: Providence is about two blocks East of Kismet.

41-39: A man's first duty is to improve his own and, later on, he must help the others.

41-40: Those who know life as a veritable rose garden have to learn how to deal with the thorns.

41-41: Applied knowledge is wise but, knowledge that is not applied is just plain dumb.

41-42: The future of every neighborhood depends on each and every neighbor.

41-43: If you are content with what you have, you don't shop enough.

41-44: People prefer peace but military people want war.

41-45: If you know where you are headed, your path will become clear.

41-46: Those who are too busy to search for success will never find any.

41-47: Those that never make a mistake, never make much.

41-48: If you have nothing to do, please do it elsewhere.

41-49: Real gardeners don't wear gloves.

41-50: The most important part of your life is now.

Good men are swept away by the grim reaper and no one from Wisconsin even cares.

CHAPTER FORTY-TWO
ITEMS 1-50

42-1: We spend the first part of our life trying to get away from our roots and, the last part, trying to get back to them.

42-2: Logic is seeing things as they really are.

42-3: Common sense is a great teacher. It allows you to do things as they should be done.

42-4: The information within books is the basis for all things undone.

42-5: If you could spank the person that is responsible for most of your problems, sitting down would be a sore experience for you.

42-6: There is always room at the top but, don't stay there too long because it is a meaner place at the top.

42-7: The best news report requires some confirmation of truth but most news reporters mix-in some of their personal bias and distortion. A few words are all that it takes.

42-8: One's character should cast a long shadow.

42-9: Wars never end soon enough and, then, they just fade away.

42-10: An ounce of truth is worth a ton of deception.

42-11: Throwing mud is losing ground.

42-12: Activity makes the difference during work or retirement.

42-13: His writing ability returned after his wife's death.

42-14: Perseverance and preparation are both required for a successful career.

42-15: The employer who trusts his employees will get more done than the employer who doesn't trust anyone.

42-16: Knowledge is like wealth. More gotten, more wanted.

42-17: Engineers are governed by the three I's; Intelligence, Imagination and Ingenuity.

42-18: Do it as you please but, please do it right.

42-19: The most popular substitute for telling the truth is the telling of lies.

42-20: Money isn't everything but, it will have to suffice until you can establish a credit card account.

42-21: The age of privacy ended with the arrival of computers and credit cards.

42-22: Peace-time and War-time represent the best and the worst of times.

42-23: To avoid credit problems, say 'yes' less often and 'no' more often.

42-24: Experience is the best teacher through experience.

42-25: Without inner peace, one will never find outer peace.

42-26: Dictatorial powers corrupt the dictator most.

42-27: Life is best spent in terms of more knowledge.

42-28: Actions speak louder than words.

42-29: Activity addresses more than inactivity does.

42-30: Without a family, a man is lost.

42-31: You can't rub wrinkles away.

42-32: Clay mud will help with the bug bites.

42-33: Bed bugs and dust mites sell more mattresses that sales people do.

42-34: Eat a banana to stop the hiccups.

42-35: It's better to belch and bear the shame than to squelch a belch and have other pain.

42-36: Eat clay dirt to cure diarrhea.

42-37: If you want to belch less, swallow less.

42-38: Willow bark helps with lower back pain.

42-39: Walk a cold away.

42-40: Swim in a muddy river to stop your fever.

42-41: To avoid the flu, just avoid people.

42-42: Headaches are caused by worrying too much.

42-43: If stung, remove the stinger first and quickly so.

42-44: If the knee is sore, use wintergreen lotion.

42-45: Witch Hazel has a terrible name but, nonetheless, it works.

42-46: Take a warm mineral bath for menstrual pain.

42-47: Eat almonds for morning sickness.

42-48: When muscles hurt, use heat.

42-49: If you have neck pain, you need a new pillow.

42-50: Eating too late causes restless legs.

Steadfast love must be praised and steadfast hatred must be abolished.

CHAPTER FORTY-THREE
ITEMS 1-50

43-1: A starch bath is good for sun-blistered skin.

43-2: A sore throat requires chamomile tea.

43-3: Witch Hazel is a good tonic for sunburn.

43-4: To avoid ear pain, don't swim in a dirty river.

43-5: For a healthy heart rhythm, stay off of the sweets.

43-6: High-heeled shoes cause jaw problems.

43-7: Clove oil is good for the toothache.

43-8: Cranberries are good for the bladder.

43-9: Bad breath is caused by cheese.

43-10: Baking soda will drive the poison away.

43-11: If you have a problem with ingrown hairs, grow a beard.

43-12: Ginger root is good for heartburn.

43-13: Tea from blackberry root cures diarrhea.

43-14: Blackheads should always be pinched but, pimples without pus should never be pinched.

43-15: Blueberries cause constipation.

43-16: Don't use vinegar on a burn.

43-17: Vinegar as a douche after having sex is thought to cause ovarian cancer.

43-18: Soak your feet in a mixture of Epsom salts and hot water.

43-19: Carrots are good for diarrhea.

43-20: It is said that cherries can cure gout.

43-21: Cold sores start with a kiss.

43-22: For chapped hands, use Crisco grease.

43-23: A plaster of raw onions will bring a boil to its head.

43-24: Ear wax will cure skin sores.

43-25: Eat fish oil for the ailing heart.

43-26: Ginseng helps with forgetfulness.

43-27: Never rub snow on a frost-burn.

43-28: Soak beans overnight or break wind during the daytime.

43-29: Sip Ginger Ale for an upset stomach.

43-30: Wear stockings to avoid foot blisters.

43-31: Eat crackers and honey for a hangover.

43-32: Eat garlic for sinus problems.

43-33: Ground oatmeal in your bath water will cure chapped skin.

43-34: More salt means more kidney stones.

43-35: Burp the baby or fight the colic.

43-36: Pick your nose and expect nose bleeds.

43-37: A thyme rinse will reduce a dandruff problem.

43-38: If you have an earache, yawn more.

43-39: It is easy to get away these days since most things are portable.

43-40: Enjoy what you have, not how much you have.

43-41: Make two people happy and one of them will be you.

43-42: Politeness is like an airplane. It gets us to where we want to be and it puts people down gracefully.

43-43: He who obeys without question has not yet learned how to reason properly.

43-44: Some alumni want the football season to last through all seasons.

43-45: There is risk in life but none in the after-life.

43-46: Judgment delayed is judgment denied.

43-47: An appeal that is granted represents judgment that is delayed.

43-48: Money makes a good worker but, a poor boss.

43-49: Money and women cause more arguments than can ever be estimated.

43-50: Never defend the reputation of a woman that you do not know.

How lovely your home is if it is a sweet home that houses both love and laughter.

CHAPTER FORTY-FOUR
ITEMS 1-50

44-1: Never give prostitutes a tip because they charge too much anyway.

44-2: Guns, knives and whiskey have caused more deaths than plagues have.

44-3: Big trouble follows the abuse by guns, knives and moonshine.

44-4: Blood-stained sidewalks need to be seen but, never cleaned.

44-5: Good conduct molds a better character.

44-6: You get very little appreciation for doing your duty especially, if that is your duty.

44-7: Self-portraits are seldom done in black and white.

44-8: If you strive to be number one, it's okay if you are number two or three.

44-9: It is all right to be old and gray at the end of your time.

44-10: A city of stone is built piece-by-piece but, destroyed in massive pieces.

44-11: An ode to women with small breasts. Anything over a mouthful is called an excess.

44-12: It takes more time to heal an injury than it does to keep one from happening.

44-13: A humble person enjoys everything more.

44-14: Our past should propel us toward our future.

44-15: Retirement should be a time of rest and enjoyment if it is done right.

44-16: Look behind or be behind. Look ahead and stay ahead.

44-17: Accept only the best and you will go without most of the worst.

44-18: The grass really is greener after a long stay in the intensive care unit of a hospital.

44-19: Justice requires immediate action. Injustice means too many delays.

43-20: Memories exist to remind us of our past.

44-21: Liberty cannot be given to anyone. It must be shared by all.

44-22: The student who is easily led will probably never lead.

44-23: Life should end after we have become what we were meant to be.

43-24: Spring reminds us of why it is so nice to live in the Country and not the City.

44-25: Where in the Country is life the cheapest, in South Brooklyn or South Los Angeles?

44-26: The ruination of our Nation will be shared by gangsters or terrorist cells.

44-27: An optimist will view each day as the best of the rest.

44-28: We buy new devices because we can't afford the cost of repairing older ones.

43-29: It is easy to see dirt on another man's face.

44-30: Humility makes you feel ordinary until you become extraordinary.

44-31: A little grit can produce a pearl.

44-32: Being broke should be a prerequisite for becoming richer.

44-33: The heart is strengthened by an uplifting experience.

44-34: Hosts can be happy twice where guests are concerned, when they come and when they go.

44-35: Before one can take, he must first undertake.

44-36: Bad weather along the way doesn't interest most parents. They just want to know that you arrived safely.

44-37: Power will flow to those that know.

44-38: When you are at the end of your rope, tie a knot and hang-on tight.

44-39: Find a Director who is mean to his Managers and he will be most humble to his Vice-Presidents.

44-40: An expert is one who has made more mistakes than most.

44-41: Responsibility finds suitable shoulders to rest upon.

44-42: You know you are good when others try to steal your thoughts.

44-43: Cut too many corners and you will run in circles.

44-44: Sometimes it pays to stick out your neck.

44-45: Between too much and too little is a happy place called just right.

44-46: Most people are as happy as they want to be.

44-47: People with problems are self-made people.

44-48: Never leave to tomorrow what you can still do today.

44-49: Today is the tomorrow that you feared yesterday.

44-50: The root of all evil is not money, it is idleness.

A man's home is his castle unless there are prison bars present.

CHAPTER FORTY-FIVE
ITEMS 1-50

45-1: Gain involves both pain and risk.

45-2: Forensic experts tell us that murder requires the elements of motive, opportunity and means. They forgot the most important element which is someone's madness.

45-3: A caring for details makes perfection more likely.

45-4: To avoid trouble later, do it right the first time.

45-5: Anything said to be complete is not yet fully completed.

45-6: The best way to get the USA going again is to get behind the USA and help.

45-7: You can't steal second base by keeping your foot on first base.

45-8: The educated man knows that fire can burn but the smarter man remembers the blisters.

45-9: To do something in a sober way is the only way.

45-10: The more complicated we are, the less effective we become.

45-11: Keep it simple and keep it worthy, stupid.

45-12: Do others better than you did for yourself.

45-13: A home run requires a good swing with a great bat.

45-14: There is no safety appliance better than the one which is located between the ears.

45-15: Always remember that the word 'American' still ends with the four important letters of 'ican'.

45-16: The word 'laboratory' is interesting. More gets done by the first five letters than by the last seven letters.

45-17: Don't try to help with the solution if you are a part of the problem.

45-18: To procrastinate is to steal time and, that makes you a thief.

45-19: Don't let your best work become your standard. Always strive for higher standards.

45-20: The root cause for most disputes is because of ignorance.

45-21: The secret of success is being better prepared.

45-22: Choose the path that is most logical and let hard work do the rest.

45-23: Good habits make living far more tolerable.

45-24: We are children only once so, after we grow older, we have to search for other explanations of our behavior.

45-25: Apathy is the one sin that should not be forgiven.

45-26: One can have some character without being educated but, one cannot become well educated without more character.

45-27: Hard work and no play-time is bad but, no work-time and too much play is worse.

45-28: The best engineers are honest, humble and logical.

45-29: Most politicians are without common sense because they are arrogant and totally dishonest.

45-30: Most politicians are corrupted by well-laundered dollars.

45-31: There is a very thin line between confidence and arrogance.

45-32: Before any work can be really great, it must first begin.

45-33: Many young people offer potential but, only the bravest gain momentum.

45-34: A good product will find some customers but, a bad product will have fewer buyers.

45-35: Side-step all of the issues and you will never make any real progress.

45-36: Life is like an abrasive wheel. It either grinds you down or polishes you up, depending upon what you are made of and which grit that you chose.

45-37: We must aspire to achieve more in the future by studying our mistakes of the past.

45-38: Little did Truman know that other Nations would, one day, bear atomic bombs.

45-39: Angry words should go unheard because they accomplish very little when heard.

45-40: Fear the power of patience.

45-41: If you made a lot of mistakes today, make less tomorrow.

45-42: The elderly might make more mistakes than others do but, they know more, don't they?

45-43: Dried milk needs water.

45-44: What happened to you and what happened to me is not the same. Would someone please explain that to our women?

45-45: Time travels at a set speed but, some of us still try to go too fast.

45-46: The most important thing to learn is how to live inside of our own skin.

45-47: Conscience gets a lot of credit that really belongs to cold feet.

45-48: A will that donates wealth to a charitable cause robs friends and relatives of their rightful inheritance.

45-49: We are most charitable with other people's money.

45-50: The best test of kinship comes at the reading of a will.

A good person will be compassionate to the needs of others and a bad person won't.

CHAPTER FORTY-SIX
ITEMS 1-50

46-1: Good health makes life on Earth a pleasure but, bad health turns life on Earth into a horrible hell.

46-2: A good feeling and useful logic is a recipe for best results.

46-3: The United Nations was organized to protect us from ourselves.

46-4: Make the most of whatever comes until it goes.

46-5: The problem with Hollywood role models is that too many people try to mimic them.

46-6: Forewarned is forearmed.

46-7: Americans are crazy because we think that anything is possible and it is.

46-8: In recent years since Reagan, there has been a stampede toward irresponsibility.

46-9: When success turns a person's head, he faces toward failure.

46-10: We have to hand it to the politician because that is where most of our tax money goes, anyway.

46-11: By hook or crook, politicians get what they want.

46-12: In any pleasure, there are always side-effects.

46-13: Slavery should exist only if the slaves consent.

46-14: True genius is the infinite capacity for handling details.

46-15: The greatest wonders of this World are men and women.

46-16: Received gifts become boring but, given gifts are never boring.

46-17: Evolution is a fine theory but, please remember, that the process is not yet finished.

46-18: Essential liberty must never be forfeited for temporary security.

46-19: Know the difference between keeping your chin up and sticking your neck out.

46-20: Don't be sold a bill of goods that is less than it should be.

46-21: Business men say that that our World is divided between two distinct parts, the developed and the developing Nations.

46-22: Christians say that the World is divided into two parts, those that believe in God and those who do not.

46-23: Christians and atheists are different but, they can be defined. The former offers us an eternal life while the latter offers us only a finite life of four score and ten, maximum.

46-24: You don't teach religion, you catch it.

46-25: Unfortunately, you are what others see.

46-26: How much you love your family is more important than how much they love you.

46-27: Unless we are our own master, we are but slaves to others.

46-28: My wife has me under contract but, I am accountable to God.

46-29: A Country can be no weaker than its faith.

46-30: Prayer, by itself, doesn't change much. Prayer changes people that pray.

46-31: If someone asks you to go the whole distance, consider what might happen when the trip is over.

46-32: I searched for my soul which I could not see. I tried to find God who eluded me. I sought my brother and found all three.

46-33: Most men worry themselves into forgotten graves. Yet, some good men forget themselves into Sainthood.

46-34: The criminal mind suffers malnutrition of another kind, not enough spiritualism.

46-35: Destroy possible enemies by making known friends.

46-36: Study truth and know God.

46-37: Reformation begins with a single convert.

46-38: Treat assets and liabilities as loyal friends who keep you safe from harm.

46-39: One's future is determined by choice and design.

46-40: What is right is far more important than who is right.

46-41: Friendship is like a checking account. You have to balance deposits and withdrawals.

46-42: Bank presidents live or die by credit or debit.

46-43: Friendship is like farming the soil, the more that you put into the soil, the more that you get out of it.

46-44: Live and let live is not enough. Live and help others to live better is best.

46-45: Always over-estimate your rival but, under-estimate yourself.

46-46: We reap what we sow.

46-47: An idea small enough to convince management is never large enough to convince the Patent Office.

46-48: Most patents are written so that they cannot be enforced.

46-49: Praise ruins more people than criticism does.

46-50: Space flight can be improved only through funded research.

The boastful should not boast. Instead, they should give praise.

CHAPTER FORTY-SEVEN
ITEMS 1-50

47-1: Even if you are but one, remember that one can always do something.

47-2: More knowledge should ensure greater happiness.

47-3: Everyone can do his part even though it is ever so small.

47-4: Habits make us what we are.

47-5: The harder you work, the luckier that you become.

47-6: Unless we produce happiness as it is being consumed, happiness becomes an endangered product.

47-7: Deep-rooted hatreds are like bad reputations. Both are difficult to remove.

47-8: A missionary is someone who wants his conscience to be your guide.

47-9: When angry, count to ten. If that doesn't help, keep counting.

47-10: Prosperity and adversity seem to be attracted to those who have the most of either one.

47-11: Conscience is heard by those who will listen.

47-12 Conscience is felt by the sensitive people.

47-13: I am grateful for many things but, having talented ancestors was most helpful.

47-14: An honest person has little trouble sleeping.

47-15: He who feels too strongly that he must improve something usually needs improvement for himself.

47-16: The older the violin, the sweeter the music.

47-17: Each of us should live our life in a manner that makes the World less difficult for others.

47-18: If nothing worthwhile was done today, then a lot of man-hours were wasted.

47-19: Shopping malls don't have penny sales.

47-20: I have very few enemies and, perhaps, only one but, having one, is more than I need.

47-21: I would rather be correct and criticized over being wrong and praised.

47-22: A needed journey through the darkest night can begin without a light. Don't let the need for a light stop that important journey.

47-23: A successful product must serve a purpose, be strong, look good and cost less.

47-24: Men with no enemies have fewer friends.

47-25: A good politician thinks twice before saying nothing of importance.

47-26: Loners who overwork need to learn how to do team work.

47-27: The best substitute for borrowing is called saved money.

47-28: Those who are best at throwing wet dirt are usually closest to the mud.

47-29: Too often, great minds run in the same gutter.

47-30: It is time to bring back the Works Progress Administration and the Civilian Concentration Corps.

47-31: To avoid the effects of famine and plague, something must be done about all of the impoverished people. Let them become 'quasi-poverished'.

47-32: Love doesn't conquer all. It also produces victims.

47-33: No great-grandfather should be classified as a failure.

47-34: In battle, it is harder to live courageously and much easier to die quickly.

47-35: What snobs need more than anything else is 48-hours in the County Jail.

47-36: Over-inflated egos could use a hard spanking.

47-37: Friends are created or destroyed by change.

47-38: The rich man has money but, the richest man has a good wife and her money.

47-39: People that anger too easily always have fewer friends.

47-40: People who fly into a rage too quickly are poor pilots.

47-41: People who can't control their temper are out-of-control.

47-42: To understand a man's problems, live one day exactly as he lives.

47-43: Knowing 'how' gets much but, knowing 'why' gets more.

47-44: To the French people: Eating cake is better than eating nothing.

47-45: Talk when you are angry and you will say words that you will regret.

47-46: The best 'do-it-yourself' theme is to think.

47-47: What we see depends upon what we seek.

47-48: Truth may commence from the brain but it starts with the heart.

47-49: Do right and never wrong but, just in case, get it in writing.

47-50: Wrong no one but write off nothing.

I have had a wonderful life. Does that mean that I will be bored in my after-life?

CHAPTER FORTY-EIGHT
ITEMS 1-50

48-1: To have a friend, you must be a friend.

48-2: If two are to remain as friends, one must be more tolerant than the other.

48-3: A squirrel in your oak tree will mean that more acorns might fall this Fall.

48-4: Trust and truth are inseparable companions.

48-5: No molecule of water in a disastrous flash flood can be held responsible.

48-6: To control yourself, use your head.

48-7: To control others, use your heart.

48-8: Living, loving, thinking and dying are tasks that we must do for ourselves.

48-9: To think about what must be done, gives untroubled sleep. To regret what you have badly done, gives a more troubled sleep.

48-10: Carpetbaggers are never allowed to enter the house.

48-11: Some people are welcome only once.

48-12: Weeds are flowers that are not fully appreciated.

48-13: The duckling that is ugly is still a duckling.

48-14: The three elements for a happy life in a crowded city involve these elements; your job, your family and your future.

48-15: In a publishing company, I prefer that they sell the books instead of trying to turn me into a book salesman when I am only the author.

48-16: An author who tries to peddle his own books is a fool for trying.

48-17: Grief should not be shared but, joy must be shared. There is too much of the former and too little of the latter.

48-18: Life is a cycle of higher achievement or lower depravation.

48-19: Causing hatred among the different classes will never nurture brotherhood.

48-20: Leadership doesn't make the Nation, good citizenship does.

48-21: If an old person's brain functions well, that person is still productive.

48-22: Limiting tenure for old teachers makes good sense to me because the mind and the body grow old together.

48-23: When I do a fault analysis, I start with myself and I work as diligently as I can.

48-24: Give without remembering and take without forgetting.

48-25: Worry is the interest that we pay today so that tomorrow's troubles might not happen.

48-26: A man sinks lowest when he sits down to plan a crime.

48-27: Tainted money is usually money that is ill-gotten or unearned.

48-28: The safest way to make money is to work for it.

48-29: When you are in an argument and you see red, stop long before you become black and blue.

48-30: Life is made more difficult without baseball and apple pie.

48-31: If you want to keep friends, stop trying to have your own way.

48-32: Research is rewarding. What begins as an experiment becomes an experience.

48-33: Our enemies are not afraid of our best fighting men. What they fear most is our technology.

48-34: Our industry and our economy do best with honesty and kindness by our leadership.

48-35: A man who is left with only honesty still offers a lot.

48-36: Pity the person who is no wiser today than yesterday.

48-37: Plan your work and work by your plan.

48-38: Owners of a company that is losing money needs an attitude adjustment long before they receive a bankruptcy judgment.

48-39: Stay with your friends if you can. After a banana leaves its bunch, it gets skinned.

48-40: Before any doctor operates on someone, a second opinion from another doctor is mandated.

48-41: There is strength in numbers, especially those on the balance sheet.

48-42: The daily grind will give you more polish if you cooperate with others.

48-43: A failure is never wasted if you learn from your experience.

48-44: For fulfillment, life gives us some allotted time and empty space with one requirement, we must use both wisely.

48-45: To kill time is to slaughter opportunities.

48-46: The one fault that is excused most often is idleness.

48-47: The happiest man is the contented one.

48-48: Working men never get enough respect.

48-49: Bravery is one human quality that guarantees others.

48-50: We grow tired of all criticisms given but, we never tire of praise that is received.

Much is said about men and too little is stated about women.

CHAPTER FORTY-NINE
ITEMS 1-50

49-1: Fear does more harm than rewards or bonuses do.

49-2: Not much is gained if something is done too quickly and improperly.

49-3: The grave digger's pride is that he starts his work while at the top.

49-4: The mortician's creed is, 'better thee than me'.

49-5: Truth, dedication and honor are required for best achievement.

49-6: Too often, opportunity looks too much like hard work.

49-7: The longer you put off doing an easy job, the harder the job becomes.

49-8: The deeper the lake, the less noise that it makes.

49-9: The best place to find a helping hand is at the end of your wrist.

48-10: The wider the lake, the greater is the pollution.

49-11: The kindest hand-out isn't related to the classroom. The best hand-out comes from your own pocket.

49-12: Don't dislike what you have to do. Like what you have to do.

49-13: The happy factor equals (How much you want) divided by (How much you have).

49-14: The money factor equals (How much you save) divided by (How much you spend).

49-15: The reality factor is the happy factor divided by the money factor.

49-16: If one can get along without more faith, then one has a faith that is good enough.

49-17: For success, always set higher standards for yourself.

49-18: Engage your brain before you start your tongue.

49-19: When limits are imposed, limitations exist.

49-20: He that lingers will languish.

49-21: It is harder to be hit from behind if you keep moving.

49-22: I admire postage stamps. They take a licking but they stick around until their job is finished.

49-23: The first postage stamps were made with a glue that contained a carcinogen. That's why I will never trust the Post Office again.

49-24: Don't look at the cause without searching for the cure.

49-25: Some journalists never know the difference between expose and exposure.

49-26: Some Presidents surround themselves with inferior associates. But, the great ones associate only with the best advisors.

49-27: Money can't buy love but, money can buy a politician.

49-28: Our past and our future are insignificant without the power to move Congress.

49-29: If you have any blackmail on our Congressmen, please share it with us because we need all of the help that we can get if we are to ever change Congress.

49-30: The strongest closing argument is to tell the truth.

49-31: Congress worked best when their income was much less than it is today.

49-32: A Congress that is strong on voter's needs will be popular but their tenure will be short because 'status quo' rules the Capitol Building in this day and age.

49-33: Will Rogers upset more Senators and Representatives than any other person during the history of our Nation. And, look what he got for his troubles, a sabotaged airplane.

49-34: If I could choose my hero, it would be Will Rogers, one of the greatest philosophers that ever lived.

49-35: The best thing about luck is that it never remains the same.

49-36: Fortunately, bad weather doesn't last very long.

49-37: In Los Angeles, I had good weather for 300-days each year. In Philadelphia, I had bad weather for 300-days each year. MORAL: Go West young people.

49-38: If the USA were shaped like a cow (as it appears to be), you would have to lift the tail to find San Francisco.

49-39: Being in a rut and being in a grave are similar except for the depth and the tenure.

49-40: If you want an army that is virtually invincible, educate the soldiers.

49-41: A humble person knows the truth about himself.

49-42: Why is parenthood always entrusted to amateurs?

49-43: Grandchildren like grandparents because grandparents are the only grown-ups that they know.

49-44: Most people are as happy as they will let themselves be.

49-45: Happiness must be rationed because it is sure a scarce commodity.

49-46: Diagrams and equations must address the needs of the people if they are to be meaningful and accepted.

49-47: I wasn't mean enough to inherit any graduate students.

49-48: Walking with someone is nice if you walk together.

49-49: The old way of walking the wife with her being twenty paces behind the husband was humiliating and offered no conversation.

49-50: Unfortunately, some people get older without becoming any better.

I searched my soul and found nothing. I looked in the mirror and saw less.

CHAPTER FIFTY
ITEMS 1-50

50-1: Veterinarians carry more fleas.

50-2: Tax consultants prefer married clients with large families.

50-3: I have no income because I am a writer. As a result, I depend on Medicare.

50-4: It is all right to be a victim of circumstance unless you are the circumstance.

50-5: When life gives you lemons, make lemonade.

50-6: We complain that rose bushes have too many thorns. Yet, we rejoice when thorny bushes have lots of roses.

50-7: Losing can never be as rewarding as winning.

50-8: Catch one fish and you will eat one meal. Teach another how to fish and you both will eat well for a lifetime.

50-9: Divorce is an attitude problem and marriage is a frame of mind.

50-10: Egoists or narcissists must never marry. If they do, they will be quickly divorced.

50-11: Losers can't be choosers.

50-12: Working hands avoid trouble better than idle hands.

50-13: Behave honorably and do not fear failure.

50-14: People without a job do not behave in a rational manner.

50-15: When a man's stomach goes empty, his mind goes blank.

50-16: Most men commit suicide because of a terminal illness.

50-17: Some men commit suicide because they can't get work.

50-18: Hemmingway committed suicide because the words wouldn't come.

50-19: This author is contemplating suicide because his books won't sell.

50-20: Whatever hits the fan is purported to be evenly distributed but, the undeserving still seem to catch more.

50-21: Once upon a time, a circus clown had two sons who worked for NASA. Neither son ever equaled the success that their father achieved.

50-22: In a crowded bar, one drunk said to another, "I used to work for NASA." To which the other drunk responded, "Didn't everyone?"

50-23: Sane men act as young boys while insane men seldom do.

50-24: We idolize love too much without loving enough.

50-25: Sex is not love, it is lust and that doesn't last long enough.

50-26: A real man's love is to take care of his wife throughout twenty-plus years of ovarian cancer.

50-27: When two get married, the fool wishes for total bliss forever while the wise one knows that trouble is just around the corner.

50-28: One way to avoid the slippery place at the top is to work farther down.

50-29: Minorities and the customers have to pay the same price for a cup of coffee.

50-30: A short sentence is no longer a proverb. Now-a-days, a short sentence is too often known as 'probation with time off for good behavior'.

50-31: In the great depression, workers wept while sluggards slept.

50-32: What communists say about welfare is this: "It is wasted money."

50-33: If you lived in Russia, you would not be alive if you were over eighty and had no family to take care of you.

50-34: Goodness is always recognized but, seldom rewarded.

50-35: I would rather live in Texas where nothing much ever happens. That beats living in the District where too much of everything happens each night.

50-36: What we have in this Country is a melting pot of individuals and no recipe.

50-37: Supreme happiness is to have been miserable just once.

50-38: Education in this Country should be treated as a war on ignorance with only one objective, to win that terrible war.

50-39: As the public views it, ethical behavior is the apparent avoidance of bad habits and improper behavior.

50-40: Those of us who are doing well were once well-taught.

50-41: When a new phrase is used in a speech, it is no longer new.

50-42: Presidents are a symbol of what is great and good about America. But, all too often, that image fades and, usually, right after an election is over.

50-43: He that believes lies shall not prosper.

50-44: A completely-free man hungers for too much.

50-45: The more that I saw of my little valley, the more that I yearned for the hills far beyond our own.

50-46: Woe be to them that read just one book unless it is the first of many that follow.

50-47: A gift that is small is better than no gift at all.

50-48: With hope, there is some chance but, without any hope, there is no chance.

50-49: The one certain thing in my life is this, I must use it before I lose it.

50-50: It would be nice if we still had a Master in every Art.

Men may know wisdom and instruction but what do they know about insight?

CHAPTER FIFTY-ONE
ITEMS 1-50

51-1: Now-a-days, we are overly concerned with the Manual Arts.

51-2: Enough is what you have after you have suffered from more than enough.

51-3: Be noble in every thought and every deed. Thereby, you have surely bought both loneliness and need.

51-4: Adversity builds what prosperity destroys.

51-5: The art of our Government being honest is a lost art.

51-6: Our Government seems to think that the best way to contain us common folks is to increase our National debt.

51-7: There is a place and means for everyone that is alive but, nobody wants to live like that.

51-8: Dangerous writers have written far more than they have read.

51-9: If your works and my works are but ripples on the sea, which of the biggest waves belong to you or to me?

51-10: Consult the elders about the way things were.

Consult the adults about the things that are.

Consult the young about the things that should be.

But, never forget to consult and do it regularly.

51-11: A drunken night makes a mournful morning.

51-12: It costs a lot to be a farmer but, it costs more if you are not one.

51-13: The bullfighter's creed is, "It's better to be bored than gored.

51-14: Readers should write more than they read.

51-15: Writers should read more than they write.

51-16: Women cry for strategic reasons. In that manner, they can plan their counter-attack.

51-17: The real struggle in life is to discover more opportunities.

51-18: Wag your tongue as much as you want but, never wave your pistol.

51-19: The future belongs to those who know how to be patient.

51-20: Our next President will be a woman. It is high time.

51-21: Better to turn back than to become lost.

51-22: All that shakes does not fall.

51-23: Are we all related because we share the same Sun?

51-24: The slower you go the farther you get.

51-25: A bad truce is better than a great battle.

51-26: The Taliban says, "This isn't over until the fat President cries for mercy."

51-27: Be aware of the wolf but, save one arm for your rifle.

51-28: In this World, not everyone with a stove can cook.

51-29: Once a word is spoken, it is no longer retrievable.

51-30: There are three expressions that hurt a bored child deeply and they are 'maybe', 'later' and 'never mind'.

51-31: Learn good things from your good teachers. The bad things that you learn are usually self-taught.

51-32: Life may be hard but, death is worse.

51-33: What good does honor serve a hungry man?

51-34: Politicians make promises that citizens have to live with.

51-35: If you are ticklish, you can laugh whenever you want.

51-36: Wash a hog as much as you want but, that hog will quickly find the mud.

51-37: A new necktie will quickly find the soup.

51-38: All shortages and recessions that are created by the politicians are always divided equally among the tax payers.

51-39: Congress never has a spending problem when using other people's money.

51-40: If you are tired of a friend, ask him for a loan of money.

51-41: Better to have a first quarrel than a final one.

51-42: A uniform commands no respect from a speeding bullet.

51-43: There are three types of people; grass cutters, well poisoners and salt miners. Which type are you?

51-44: Some people think that 'out-of-chaos' comes order. Others say that 'out-of-chaos' defines chaos. What say you?

51-45: Even if my wife is a hypochondriac, don't let me become a worse 'pill' than I am already.

51-46: Successful people are the only ones who profess to be a self-made person. What about their Mothers? Mothers do have a lot to do with their son's career, don't they?

51-47: Beware of the sheep that wears a wolf's clothing.

51-48: Help someone to 'get-on' today. Don't keep telling them where they can 'get-off'.

51-49: I am grateful for my wife's many faults. Without them, she might have married Bobby Haggard from Clark County.

51-50: We never get too old to avoid doing something stupid.

Wisdom seeks recognition in the streets and among all of the tall buildings.

CHAPTER FIFTY-TWO
ITEMS 1-50

52-1: Don't believe what you hear but, believe what you say.

52-2: Some of our critics are using the only talent that they have, pity them.

52-3: All it takes to make a mountain out of a molehill is to use a lot of dirt.

52-4: The greatest thing that education ever taught was to teach people how to write checks.

52-5: I was better than Nolan Ryan. I never allowed any earned runs. No one ever got any hits off of me. I never made any balks. My lifetime batting average was over 0.310. I played third base and he wasn't good enough for that position.

52-6: This is the one gift that needs to be wrapped, the gift of gab.

52-7: If we reap what we sow, pray for a drought.

52-8: Insisting is not a substitute for persisting.

52-9: Minorities that only react will seldom act.

52-10: The not-so-obvious may someday be understood but, when will we understand the obvious?

52-11: Bad work with good intentions is better than good work with bad intentions.

52-12: Wise persons are silent too often because silence is considered wise.

51-13: Talk is cheap and wise people rarely buy into it.

52-14: Happiness may be what we want but, we must avoid too much of it.

52-15: Why give working people more 'leisure' time when they can't afford the 'off-time' that they already have?

52-16: One with enough money is never without but, one without enough money is seldom with.

52-17: One lie begets others.

52-18: If children are just a little bit dishonest, why must adults be more dishonest?

52-19: Pride comes from doing a difficult task very well.

52-20: Evil spelled backwards is the word 'live'.

52-21: In some homes, the legal age for drinking beer is five-years of age.

52-22: Introducing young children to alcohol is something that evil people do.

52-23: White lies become much blacker with age.

52-24: The arrogance of youth is exceeded only by the arrogance of old age.

52-25: When I was young, I used the week to recover from the weekend. Now that I am old, I use the weekend to recover from the week.

52-26: If we try to keep up with the Jones's, the IRS will soon catch us in the act.

52-27: Adam and Eve were lucky because they by-passed teething, croup and earaches.

52-28: The same old stories from an old storyteller age more than he does.

52-29: Ninety-some percent of all people consider themselves to be above average.

52-30: Youth is when a man feels just great all of the time.

Maturity is when a man needs a day or two before he feels as good as ever.

Old age is when you get out of bed and know that it gets worse thereafter.

52-31: Too many Parsons view the World through stained-glass windows.

52-32: Those who live by telling lies will, one day, lie and quit living.

52-33: The goal for successful politicians is to pass enough legislation that will keep most voters too poor to run for any elections.

52-34: Government endures if law-abiding citizens abide.

52-35: Let us hope that what happened in Boston stays in Boston.

52-36: If science is so great, why can't scientists tell me when to leave my umbrella at home?

52-37: If early a country boy, then later, a country man.

52-38: No one appreciates home like the homeless.

52-39: The USA is best evaluated if you are living in Europe and reading an English newspaper.

52-40: The only thing that male executives have in common with working men is zippers.

52-41: Spell-check isn't enough for a good writer. He needs to always check to see if he _ _ _ _ any words out of his composition.

52-42: All laws are meaningless without enforcement.

52-43: Students like the easy teacher best but, graduates respect the hard teachers most.

52-44: The best speaker knows when to quit.

52-45: Some of the best black men have white on top.

52-46: Political promises don't fill an empty food closet.

52-47: Politicians can teach you everything that they know in ten seconds.

52-48: Youth is when we know too little and old age is when we know too much.

52-49: Politicians ought to do worthwhile things. Instead, they are too concerned with what's worth-their-while.

52-50: Movies are interesting. You enter the theater with the hope that it will be a good one but, you leave with the hope that you will someday see a better one.

Make your ear attentive to wisdom and incline your heart toward understanding.

CHAPTER FIFTY-THREE
ITEMS 1-50

53-1: Americans have but two real obligations, to pay taxes and to die.

53-2: What is the real difference between a white supremacist and a black supremacist? Not much, actually.

53-3: He that makes money from a crime is the greater criminal.

53-4: If something can be counted, it counts.

53-5: Trouble tells us what we are.

53-6: It is easy to find fault but, harder to give praise.

53-7: He that does little does less.

53-8: Bad writers make the best critics.

53-9: Mean people have more fear.

53-10: Culture improves.

53-11: Curiosity and imagination will keep you from being bored.

53-12: Health, happiness and your career makes the good life.

53-13: People will forfeit their rights before they will give up their bad habits.

53-14: Between cradle and grave, we experience danger.

53-15: The one thing that is unique about life is death.

53-16: The borrower becomes a slave to the lender.

53-17: Today, decent people still exist but, they are harder to find.

53-18: In this maddening World, people double-bolt their doors at night.

53-19: Final decisions rarely remain that way.

53-20: The marathon isn't over until the last runner shows.

53-21: Love is popular because other emotions are worse.

53-22: The right to free speech works in this Country because listeners have the right to listen or not listen.

53-23: If you must be dependent, depend on yourself.

53-24: Many things desired and a few things feared is a stage called youth.

53-25: It is wrong to say that everything bad and good is God's will.

53-26: The wicked one below has much to say about our choices.

53-27: At the end of the day, get some rest and then start over.

53-28: Never stain wet wood.

53-29: You don't have to be close, to be close.

53-30: It takes a genius to create remarkable new ideas but, it takes a good worker to make those new ideas work efficiently.

53-31: Deeds say more than words can promise.

53-32: Don't tell your children too much 'no-no'. Instead, give your children more 'know-know'.

53-33: If you have intelligence and like to be in control, avoid owning cats.

53-34: The trouble with being unemployed is that you are denied many things that you want. The trouble with being employed is that you are unable to own everything that you want.

53-35: We blame the previous generations for today's problems rather than our current generation. Isn't that convenient?

53-36: Prosperity is when the dollar stays stateside but, inflation exists when the dollar goes overseas.

53-37: Truth is always befuddled by our memories.

53-38: I have a save-button for my computer but, I need one in my brain.

53-39: A warranty period is that time which exists just prior to a failure.

53-40: Best friends are those that sanction my actions.

53-41: Where four-letter words are concerned, we never have enough love or cash.

53-42: There are two things that I respect most highly, my good wife and my PhD degree.

53-43: Smarter people make the same mistake but once.

53-44: I love my Country but, I hate my Government.

53-45: A return to your hometown is vexing. You can find your old house but, everything else seems different.

53-46: Anyone can believe what they hear. The real trick is in knowing what to believe.

53-47: Don't worry about the World until someone starts building something big enough to hold all of our animals.

53-48: Good people are uncomfortable without self-respect but, bad people are comfortable with no respect.

53-49: Being great, good and happy doesn't just happen. You have to make it happen.

53-50: Only you can fight your own fights.

Drive on the highway made by good, strong men and be mindful of their labor.

CHAPTER FIFTY-FOUR
ITEMS 1-50

54-1: Success is not caused by chance. Success is caused by choice and dedication.

54-2: Like what you do but, make adjustments when necessary.

54-3: Do at some other time what you cannot do at this time. Just don't forget to do it.

54-4: Most honest, hard-working people with good self-respect have already attained success but, there is always room for more.

54-5: Honest hard working people are still around but, they are harder to find.

54-6: Enjoy your work but, work for more enjoyment.

54-7: Some people work to live while others live to work.

54-8: One plan is never enough. Have back-up plans.

54-9: The best justification for young engineers is that machines become obsolete and old engineers disappear.

54-10: Education is expensive but it does pay-off.

54-11: Make next year more productive.

54-12: Do a task today which you could not find time for yesterday.

54-13: Stay in touch with friends so that they may not become forgotten.

54-14: Forget the argument but long remember the reconciliation.

54-15: Tell stories for those who will listen and write stories for those who will read.

54-16: The best medicine for recovery requires a strong faith.

54-17: Laugh at that which deserves laughter.

54-18: Pity those who need pity.

54-19: Nobody takes advantage of you if you don't allow it.

54-20: Experience is what you get when you don't get what you want.

54-21: The loudest squeak gets the most grease.

54-22: Soft answers accomplish more than hard answers do.

54-23: Free yourself of debt for a debt-free life.

54-24: Today's World has too much ill-will and resentment.

54-25: Patronize young children so that they will become better patrons.

54-26: Try harder and, if that doesn't work, try your hardest.

54-27: Lead by giving a good example.

54-28: When only your best will do, do it.

54-29: If we are to teach more, we need more good teachers, not new buildings.

54-30: Share your good experiences with others and keep your bad experiences to yourself.

54-31: Stay in touch with family and friends so that they are not strangers.

54-32: Don't mix fact and fiction.

54-33: Don't make the problem bigger than it already is.

54-34: Good deeds may be punished but, bad deeds will always be punished.

54-35: Accentuate the positive, eliminate the negative, latch onto the affirmative and, do not mess with me.

54-36: Aggrandize solutions, not problems.

54-37: Don't work without thinking and don't shoot from the lips.

54-38: Words that must be eaten are hard to digest.

54-39: Be kind and save time for other people.

54-40: Compliments ought to be paid without an invoice being sent.

54-41: Human beings almost defy gravity when they receive an up-lifting experience.

54-42: Don't just think about things. Think things through.

54-43: Some injustices need to be pardoned but, most don't.

54-44: Spray paint into the wind and eat paint.

54-45: Don't talk more and listen less. Instead, listen more and talk less.

54-46: It is easy to be mean but hard to be kind.

54-47: Be truthful. When you are wrong, admit it and, if you don't know, say so.

54-48: Saying that you are sorry, makes you a better man.

54-49: Don't toot your own horn too much and honor others when honors are due.

54-50: Do praiseworthy things if you want to receive praise.

Loyalty and faithfulness go a long way but, be your own man.

CHAPTER FIFTY-FIVE
ITEMS 1-50

55-1: Know other viewpoints before you form your own.

55-2: Nothing is ever completely one-way.

55-3: Perfection does not exist and fuses still blow.

55-4: Paradise is not the sole property of the islands.

55-5: Don't demand from others what you will not demand of yourself.

55-6: Back-off only if you must.

55-7: Never laugh at your own jokes.

55-8: If you desire friends, try being one first.

55-9: If you need help, don't hesitate to ask for it.

55-10: Genealogy makes the ultimate discovery that we are each related.

55-11: America doesn't need better teachers or new buildings. What they need most is to find ways in which to get the parents more involved.

55-12: A parent that asks a school teacher to baby-sit her children leaves much to be desired.

55-13: Avoid those that do not make a contribution to the sum of total knowledge.

55-14: Risk should not be managed. Risk needs to be massaged.

55-15: If something good is to be done, one is obligated to try.

55-16: Spirit plus attitude is the fuel that makes things happen.

55-17: Declare war on poverty, ignorance and lies.

55-18: Lies are told but, truths are demonstrated.

55-19: Your thanks should be expressed, not suppressed.

55-20: Too often, short people long to be appreciated while long people are left short.

55-21: Read something good and spread the goodness.

55-22: Poor fiction may upset your stomach and poison your mind.

55-23: Old sayings are always fashionable to the younger set.

54-24: If not you, who? If, not today, when?

55-25: Pornographic materials should be exiled to the garbage dump.

55-26: Be brave until all danger has left the area.

55-27: All you really have is you.

55-28: Eat better and think better.

55-29: The human body was designed to inhale air, not cigarette smoke or drugs.

55-30: Good habits can be controlled while bad habits cannot.

55-31: The trouble with our young kids of today is that most of them have become too fond of their own image, that disease is known as narcissism.

55-32: It would be a better World if all libraries had 95% of their book collection on loan.

55-33: Litter is tossed mostly by the 'ill-liter-ates',

55-34: These days, not many people will stoop to pick up pennies from where they lie. How can we be having a recession when so many people are throwing their money away?

54-35: Don't be phony because people can see through that as if it were window glass.

55-36: Know that every living thing is part of the miracle called life.

55-37: Re. word games, what do these words have in common: plain, play, clad, clan, clap, flee, glad, kneel, clue, dole, feel, fled, flew, blow, blob, cloy, clog, clot, duel, club, floe, glum, glut, howl and slow? Answer: knock the 'L' out of each and you have another word of a different meaning.

55-38: I've been sucking the hind tit for too long now.

55-39: Have the smallest waist size that you can.

55-40: Smile because someone is always watching.

55-41: Her bra size accentuates more than the rest.

55-42: Three words of maximum effect are, 'I love you'.

55-43: One word of minimum appeal is 'no'. Likewise, one word of maximum appeal is 'yes'.

55-44: One word of great significance is the small word 'if'.

55-45: People who are loved are truly blessed.

55-46: Never try to live tomorrow before it ever arrives.

55-47: We spend too much time on preparation and organization. We need to spend more time on action.

55-48: Leaders act and followers react.

55-49: Treat each day as an irreplaceable gift.

55-50: Death is the only guarantee that life can offer.

If you treasure my words, make your ears attentive to their wisdom.

CHAPTER FIFTY-SIX
ITEMS 1-50

56-1: Make today count more than yesterday did.

56-2: Forget yesterday. It is already history.

56-3: Look forward to tomorrow as another opportunity.

56-4: What young people need in the USA is exactly what Europe has had for centuries, a functional apprenticeship program.

56-5: If we can't control the inner city, how will we protect the outer city?

56-6: An urban criminal will never become urbane so conversion of the criminal is neither cost attractive nor practical.

56-7: Crime will never cease until after prisons become worse than cheap hotels or run-down neighborhoods.

56-8: Criminals have no rights and everyone needs to know that.

56-9: In the old days, hungry people found work even if it was picking peas. Nowadays, hungry persons have discovered that prisons are pleasant sanctuaries.

56-10: Don't love one child more than the other children. If you do, change your ways.

56-11: If you have to choose between your children, care most about the sickest child.

56-12: Feed the runt good food and watch him grow.

56-13: Whenever a child visits, kneel down to his level and make him feel wanted.

56-14: Be as snug as a bug in a rug.

56-15: In Congress today, we have too many characters that resemble 'tweedledom' and 'tweedledee' people.

56-16: Always say goodbye to a child in a manner that he or she will remember.

56-17: If you want your children to notice you, sit down and try to take a rest.

56-18: Every new birth could be the return of Jesus so every abortion could be the modern crucifixion of Jesus.

56-19: Men and women may make babies but, babies make families.

56-20: Little boys grow up to become big boys but, great grandfathers are the biggest boys of all.

56-21: Small children make their parents grow up.

56-22: I love little children best before they become individuals.

56-23: Be best, not pests.

56-24: Most problems could be solved if we threw enough money at it.

56-25: Smaller children solve small problems best because they are still innocent.

56-26: Critics teach us how to find fault in others.

56-27: Being hostile teaches us how to fight.

56-28: Ridicule causes shyness.

56-29: Shame causes guilt.

56-30: Tolerance teaches us how to be patient.

56-31: Encouragement gives us confidence.

56-32: Praise makes us appreciate what needs to be appreciated.

56-33: Being fair teaches us justice.

56-34: Security instills good faith.

56-35: Approval fuels self-esteem.

56-36: Rejection builds barriers.

56-37: Bias makes enemies.

56-38: Love must be understood if it is to be endured.

56-39: Harsh words are seldom mended.

56-40: If the town neglects its children, the children will neglect the town.

56-41: Childhood reveals the blooming adult just as sunrise will unveil the day.

56-42: Children learn best by identification so, be a role model.

56-43: The coldest silence ever felt is when your children leave home.

56-44: The warmest noise you will ever hear is when the prodigal child returns home.

56-45: Children will share their infections much quicker than their toys.

56-46: Spare the belt and spoil the child.

56-47: Dogs that wag their tails are ambassadors of good will.

56-48: Dogs that show their teeth and growl are like soap opera villains and bullies.

56-49: The boldest puppy of the litter gets more attention.

56-50: God was not satisfied with Adam so, he created Eve. After two failed prototypes, God turned to the pursuit of other more successful ventures.

Accept my words of wisdom and the years of your life will become plentiful.

CHAPTER FIFTY-SEVEN
ITEMS 1-50

57-1: The soldier's lament: It is more fun to create children than to slay enemy soldiers.

57-2: Have as much intercourse as you can with clean women because, at the end of the day, you won't be able to perform.

57-3: The impregnation process is the grandest form of entertainment.

57-4: Slam, bam and thank you ma'am is reserved for insensitive men.

57-5: If parents were better playwrights, then children might become the best play.

57-6: Children who play under the Sun are actors in the best play ever done.

57-7: Dead soldiers should have more respect because, in the end, they were useful, worthwhile and obedient men.

57-8: A wishbone will not suffice where a strong backbone is required.

57-9: Know when to be brave and when to be smart.

57-10: He that knows himself is most knowledgeable.

57-11: Fate is kind. It brings fulfillment.

57-12: Make your wish upon a star and that will make you better than you are.

57-13: Know when to be aggressive or yielding.

57-14: If you must travel, travel with the best.

57-15: Hearts ought to be pure and goals should be high.

57-16: Master yourself before competing with others.

57-17: Know when to laugh and remember how to cry.

57-18: Strive for a better future and learn from the past but, always make the best of now.

57-19: Have a sense of humor and an awareness of sorrow but, moreover, be humble.

57-20: Reduce all that you can to its common denominator.

57-21: Dedicated study reduces complex matters to a lower state where more is understood.

57-22: An open mind leads to wisdom while a closed mind fuels ignorance.

57-23: A son that succeeds has a father whose life was well spent.

57-24: Find out what's important in your life. Only then, will you find the time to write.

57-25: When our contributions diminish, our obligations seem to become larger.

57-26: Never forsake the dreams of your middle years as they are more productive.

57-27: Let no person ridicule my heritage. It may not be the best but, it is mine.

57-28: Old people are wiser if they understand young people.

57-29: We elders preach 'Once upon a time'. The youngsters of today say, 'What's happening? That's not a generation gap. That is the glorified past versus the confused present.

57-30: The destiny of too many Nations is decided by the politicians and their soldiers while ordinary people are forced to serve without complaining.

56-31: Everybody wants to be young, healthy and famous.

57-32: Fame is like being at the top of the mountain, which is a slippery place.

57-33: Everyone seeks recognition.

57-34: Live life properly and you won't be spending a lot of time repeating yourself.

57-35: Live life improperly and you will have to do a lot of repair work.

57-36: Teenagers are folks that like possessions better than criticisms.

57-37: The men that died in World War II died for me so that I could be free. I must always remember what they did for me.

57-38: Try to make something worthy out of your life.

57-39: Once is enough to be youthful. Who could stand being that for a whole lifetime?

57-40: When we can no longer help the young, we are obsolete and we become an obstacle in their way.

57-41: A teenager is lost somewhere between childhood and marriage.

57-42: Nobody should remain immature for too long.

57-43: The smart ones are young and immature just once and briefly so.

57-44: The older ones say, 'you must' while the youngest ask 'why'?

57-45: Indefinite maturity may sound like fun when you are young but, as you grow older, it becomes quite dull at about thirty-something.

57-46: Youth is the time for preparation. Maturity is the time for improvement. Old age is the time for letting go.

57-47: What scares me the most about my own teenagers is that they remind me too much of me.

57-48: Teenagers don't believe in Santa Claus and, they no longer ask where they came from.

57-49: Teenagers of today prefer to come and go as they damn well please.

57-50: Parenthood's toughest years are when their children are between the ages of twelve and nineteen.

Walk in my shoes for one mile and you will realize what I feel.

CHAPTER FIFTY-EIGHT
ITEMS 1-50

58-1: When children grow to between 12 and 19, their change is only seven years. However, their parents do age by an amount which is about twice that.

58-2: A good education will always exist if the student understands mankind but, knows his religion better.

58-3: Immaturity is that part of life when we know that we will never be as dumb as our parents.

58-4: Maturity is that part of life when we know that we were wrong about our parents, all along.

58-5: My daughter and my wife have one thing in common. They both know how to use the telephone quite well. However, neither one of them have mastered the fine art of ending a telephone conversation.

58-6: Your best chance in life will not occur without preparation and study.

58-7: You must try to learn one new thing each day if you are to become erudite.

57-8: Any age is the right age to improve your life.

58-9: A smart ass is well informed about most everything that his friends do not know or will not study.

58-10: Parents want their children to have what they never had, straight 'A's' and a good 'deportment rating' on their report card.

58-11: The World cannot long survive without children. So, don't practice birth control. Just take care of those that are born.

58-12: The tossing of girl babies into the Yangtze River was pollution at its highest level.

58-13: Having a good child is an accident of sorts but, turning them into adults requires hard work.

58-14: Cosmetics were invented during the middle ages and they are still being used to hide the effects of being middle-aged.

58-15: As a young engineer, you start by getting ahead. As a middle-aged engineer, you try to hang on. As an old engineer, you look for a new profession.

58-16: A youngster thinks that life will last forever. A middle-aged person wonders why time has gone by so fast. An older person worries about how little is left.

58-17: I don't resent growing old. I do dislike the fact that everything I do takes much too long.

58-18: Adolescence is being both young and silly. Old age is just being silly.

58-19: As an old person, I have but one advantage over the baby-boomers. I have been both young and old while they have been only young. Pity the poor rascals.

58-20: The only advantage of growing old in today's society is that some merchants will give me a senior citizen discount.

58-21: As a veteran, I do get a military discount at certain stores if I wear my lucky cap about the 'Old Hickory' division.

58-22: Teach your kids to compete in their World. But, never encourage them to join any gangs in South LA.

58-23: Remember that competition in your child's World isn't identical to that for your own World.

58-24: Being a grandfather is a massive responsibility where you have to teach your grandchildren about the old ways. Why should you do that? Because no one else can.

58-25: If grandmother takes her grandkids to church, then everyone profits more.

58-26: Too many people believe that more is better.

58-27: If twenty is the young age of youth and forty is the old age of youth, then sixty is the young age of old age and 80 is the old age of old age. But what can be said about being 100? Is it the old, old age of old age?

58-28: One is as young as their dreams or as old as their actions.

58-29: If you want to become poor, open a restaurant or sell used cars.

58-30: The initial goal of labor unions was to keep workers from being overworked and mistreated. In this they have become most successful. Nowadays, most labor unions are unemployed and the Third World laughs about it.

58-31: Outsourcing has become a large problem for which there is no solution.

58-32: Perhaps, we should triple the price of rice, corn and wheat which they purchase from us. Some critics would call that dangerous but I would call it revenge.

58-33: Never judge an employee by what he or she is paid.

57-34: Most employees are judged by what they cost.

58-35: Women are always paid less than men and this is because they will take it.

58-36: Perhaps, women should sing that old song, "We're not gonna take it, No, we ain't gonna take it, We're not gonna take it anymore."

58-37: The upper half lives off of the interest that the lower half pays.

58-38: When people buy things, they complain very little. When they get gifts, they complain more.

58-39: No debt is due at the right time.

58-40: The worst part of any letter is these two words, 'Amount Due'.

58-41: This democracy system won't function properly until we get everyone a job.

58-42: One third of our people contribute while two-thirds receive.

58-43: An honest politician averages just one term in office.

57-44: In the USA, we emphasize 'us' too much.

58-45: From what I have seen and heard, it ought to be called the Divided States of America.

58-46: America does not stand by its citizens in the same resolute manner as it supports the American Corporations.

58-47: Non-profit corporations can do things which are illegal for other ordinary Corporations.

58-48: It bothers me that some people can do things which are illegal and immoral yet still classified as legal.

58-49: Our problem is not what the dollar is worth. Our problem is that we print too many dollars.

58-50: Medical people say that money is unclean and a known source of communicable diseases. Is that why doctors try to collect as many dollars as they can so that they can evaluate our infected green paper?

From the lips of a loose woman drips honey and her words are sweeter than wine.

CHAPTER FIFTY-NINE
ITEMS 1-50

59-1: In the old days, a company grew larger by selling better products to more consumers. In this day and age, a company grows larger by selling more stock to more investors.

59-2: The stock market report causes more torment than bad food does.

59-3: The more successful lawyer writes the more confusing writ.

59-4: Any written thing that you cannot understand was probably written by a lawyer.

59-5: If, you can't do anything else, practice law.

59-6: The more successful lawyers have no conscience.

59-7: Lawyers are too dedicated to procedure.

59-8: Very often, the guilty party is released on a technicality.

59-9: In a courtroom, lawyers are never sworn in and there is a good reason for that to be the case.

59-10: Once an innocent party was incarcerated because her lawyer followed the right procedure wrongly. Why must we follow so many procedures anyway?

59-11: I was in court when a case was being argued about 'The Uniform Code'. One side presented the opinion that his learned opponent did not follow the requirements of Rule Number Nine. The judge responded by saying, "He pleaded according to each of the eight rules. What does rule number nine address"? The other side quickly stated, "Everything else." And, the courtroom was filled with much cynicism and laughter." Guess who won that case? It was the side that made the Judge laugh, that's who.

59-12: I never cared for the statement, "Let the Law takes its course." It is more accurate to say, "Let the law take, of course."

59-13: In one of my college lectures, I said, "We need to get rid of all the unethical types. Immediately, all of my students left the classroom.

59-14: Lawyers do not like clients who have no money.

59-15: Clients with money do not like lawyers.

59-16: Lawyers and bankers seldom retire but they do get pardoned.

59-17: Estate lawyers forget that it is our will and final testament. It should never involve their will for investment schemes.

59-18: Whistle when you pass a cemetery.

59-19: Taxes should be more affordable, like a zero-based budget.

59-20: Our treasury system is unique. It is a 'put' and 'take' operation where taxpayers 'put' some in but, politicians 'take' more out.

59-21: Ignorance is like mayonnaise, it spreads easily.

59-22: Congressmen are allowed to visit countries around the World while taxpayers have to foot the bill.

59-23: There are lots of different subjects to study at the University because the educators believe that there is safety in numbers.

59-24: Americans are better educated than ever before but, Americans are worse off now than ever before. Is there a correlation here?

59-25: I know one university that used the same textbooks for more than forty years. Is there any wonder why all of the graduates each knew the same thing?

59-26: A wise graduate never ventures very far from his field of interest. Those that do leave their major field of study fail more quickly.

59-27: Education pays enough if we pay enough for the education.

59-28: The less you know, the harder you need to work.

59-29: The more you know, the less you want to work.

59-30: The shortest path to the brain must involve the eye rather than the ear because students learn more from illustrations and charts than they do by listening to eloquent speeches.

59-31: Education does not do enough for our morals because the smartest graduates usually become the biggest crooks.

59-32: Sum and substance customers get exactly what they deserve.

59-33: Young people never make the mess that they inherit. They just inherit the riches.

59-34: Our knowledge of the unknown is not increasing fast enough. Ask the nice folks that are terminally ill.

59-35: Kentucky teaches basketball best and Texas A&M teaches football best but I have taught athletes at both schools who could not read nor write.

59-36: One can be associated with a fine university for a great number of years without knowing the people that work there. And, when you get to really know them, it is time to leave. Highway 6 runs both North and South.

59-37: Yale graduates are beer drinkers from way back. They have always instructed their bartenders, I'll have a mug of "Y" ale.

59-38: History must be dedicated to actual facts because historians aren't.

59-39: The smartest man I ever knew taught himself to read using wallpaper made from newspapers. He spent a lot of hours in our outhouse.

59-40: Travel tempers testiness and shortens one's temper.

59-41: A scientist bends the laws of nature to fit his own theories.

59-42: An engineer follows the laws of nature to make things work.

59-43: There are two ways to get smarter. Read more and surround yourself with people who are smarter than you are.

59-44: We used to judge according to deeds that were done but, now we judge too much by appearances.

59-45: More said means more arguments but, less said is still deemed better.

59-46: It is said that Confucius said so much while too many listened to him too little.

59-47: No one appreciates our Country more than the illegal immigrants do. Some of them are necessary for the robbing of stores and the home invasions.

59-48: It is odd that European tourists now come to America for the buying of cheap manufactured goods. Just a few years ago, it was the other way around.

59-49: The rich and famous are dedicated to money. The poor and humble are encouraged to remain poor and humble.

59-50: Fun is easily defined. It is going somewhere and doing something enjoyable.

Drink water from your own cistern and your water will be blessed.

CHAPTER SIXTY
ITEMS 1-50

60-1: Traffic wouldn't be so bad if the roadways accepted only those vehicles that were completely paid for.

60-2: Mexico is a good neighbor during the daytime. However, that is not the case after nightfall. Ask the people who live in El Paso.

60-3: Texas merchants like Mexican customers because they are such good daytime spenders.

60-4: The World has too many churches with too many preachers that are not properly qualified.

60-5: It has been said that Russians are hard to read. That's because they are so cold and hungry.

60-6: Why does a woman cry more when she is happy?

60-7: Most men have three pursuits, women, money and happiness.

60-8: If women insist on living like a man, then they will have to start acting like one.

60-9: When women start acting like men, I don't look forward to the outcome.

60-10: Fiction sells better than non-fiction because, with the former, the writer has more leeway.

60-11: Without friends, we are deprived of much too much.

60-12: Truth and harmony must exist primarily in Heaven because there's very little of either to be seen on Earth.

60-13: The most common malady among humans is greed.

60-14: Never criticize something that you don't understand and never criticize someone that you don't know.

60-15: Success is measured by satisfaction which is achieved.

60-16: The World would be a greater place if each of us were as great as we think we are.

60-17: If you want to find out about the truth about someone, speak to the relatives of that person.

60-18: Never forget those people who helped you to become the success that you are.

60-19: Never proceed if you are unsure.

60-20: Doing well and meaning well are not identical.

60-21: Pronounce clearly but, don't denounce too loudly.

60-22: Remarks that hurt are directly proportional to the truth.

60-23: Praise and criticism should very indirectly.

60-24: New is not always better and old is never completely out of style.

60-25: Any new day that we are permitted to have is a great old day.

60-26: If malice is not in your heart, it won't be in your head.

60-27: A dollar taken is a dollar given.

60-28: Most job offers means that another person was fired.

60-29: When a company becomes 'lean and mean', fewer employees exist.

60-30: Productivity declines when an employee's motivational skills diminish.

60-31: Wish for something that doesn't cause another person pain.

60-32: It is easier to criticize than to apologize.

60-33: Critics are paid to criticize so don't expect praise.

60-34: Critics grow worse with time because, with each new review, they feel the need to find something new that's wrong. After a few years of this attitude, approval becomes an extinct entity.

60-35: Teachers grow more difficult with time because they feel the need to make the course harder each time that the subject is offered.

60-36: Today's classroom education works best if we have one excellent teacher and a very good enforcer who is good with his fists. Usually, the enforcer is the young man who is banging the teacher.

60-37: Progress is best measured by happiness.

60-38: Civilization will cease to exist if human rights continue to be abused.

60-39: Nobody is completely satisfied about everything.

60-40: If we know more about knowledge, our knowledge will expand.

60-41: If our knowledge contracts, we will know less.

60-42: Never say never or forever.

60-43: A civilized society cannot exist if everyone is dissatisfied.

60-44: We need to be a Nation that exports terrorists.

60-45: Why must we make the terrorists happy in Boston and other cities?

60-46: Prosperity creates problems.

60-47: As it turns out, the Native Americans were more civilized than we are.

60-48: Our current citizens are unhappy, dissatisfied and too dependent on the Government.

60-49: Treasures gained by wickedness will never profit very much.

60-50: Ask me nothing about political wars because I do not understand the need for them.

Isn't it wonderful that every woman is different?

CHAPTER SIXTY-ONE
ITEMS 1-50

61-1: We ought to send more money to Counties, not Countries.

61-2: Bring all our Soldiers home and leave the pagans be.

61-3: The only way that America can ever recover is, if everyone gets involved.

61-4: In the USA, there is no excuse for hunger.

61-5: Missionaries go where businessmen will soon follow.

61-6: The most relevant work in all literature is the Bible.

61-7: Newspapers will be fair when they print both births and obituaries.

61-8: The good die young because they are not well prepared and cannot cope.

61-9: The dead soldier who was wounded in the back was, most likely, a victim of friendly fire.

61-10: The dead soldier who was wounded in the front probably 'zigged' when he should have' zagged'.

61-11: In California, everybody shakes, especially when the ground moves.

61-12: Native Californians argue that the moving ground keeps the trash in Arizona.

61-13: Why did Howard Hughes move to Las Vegas? ANSWER: He wanted oceanfront property.

61-14: Use sweet words because they are easier to eat.

61-15: There is no dignity in a wrongful death.

61-16: When I wear my Army hat, cute women thank me for my services. The trouble is that I don't remember servicing them.

61-17: I must be famous because everyone is thanking me for not smoking. Am I the Marlboro man or not?

61-18: I don't own beachfront property because Texas is due for a tsunamis.

61-19: Please God, bless America before it is too late.

61-20: Some of us make a good impression when the Dentist makes a good mold.

61-21: Judge people by how much they will be missed. Right now, my last remaining aunt stands at the top of my list at 94-years of age.

61-22: Too often, a life well spent meant a large debt for the heirs.

61-23: Never judge a New Year's Day by its beginning.

61-24: People that live right die best.

61-25: The challenge of good living is to die satisfied.

61-26: With our current medical costs, no one can afford to get sick.

61-27: Nobody wants to die because too much is still unfinished.

61-28: Death means a new beginning, not an ending.

61-29: The most attention that I ever received was when I had my first major surgery. Friends and former students came from both near and far.

I recovered from the surgery but, I still haven't recovered from that huge medical bill.

61-30: If disease doesn't kill you, your medical costs will.

61-31: Now that the insurance companies are covering less, more people are dying.

61-32: A pessimist in Washington, DC might argue that the old should be allowed to die gracefully and it is wrong to give them medical service in their final years. But, such critics have forgotten one major point. If we are invaded, my guns will be used to defend me.

61-33: Old soldiers never die, they just fade away.

61-34: My only sister died at birth and she is still with me, my Norma Lee.

61-35: Hollywood stars do not decorate the streets of Heaven and they never will because they never behaved as Christians do.

61-36: Most of our dreamers come from the little-dreamed-of places, like Hazard, Kentucky.

61-37: Nothing should be lost forever but a lot does fall through the cracks.

61-38: England will never appreciate Ireland as the Irish do.

61-39: Reason says that death is the final season.

61-40: Fortunate children have a Mother's love which never fails or falters.

61-41: Best things are the nearest and dearest things.

61-42: After storms, we have sunshine.

61-43: Life is best when the Blue North winds end.

61-44: Ask for enough but, don't ask for all.

61-45: Love grows stronger if it is shared.

61-46: Fathers are not well understood unless we thank them as we should.

61-47: Be a guardian and a guide to everyone that is on your side.

61-48: Give thanks each day to avoid Harm's way.

61-49: Be most thankful that you are still able to give thanks.

61-50: Fill your heart with thanksgivings and your stomach will never suffer on Thanksgiving Day.

The memory of a righteous deed is ever lasting.

CHAPTER SIXTY-TWO
ITEMS 1-50

62-1: Quit supposing and start sufficing.

62-2: Success is in the knowing that someone cares.

62-3: No day is too dark.

62-4: No burden is too heavy.

62-5: In this life, one cannot see God but, you can feel his presence.

62-6: The more that you laugh, the less that you regret.

62-7: The more that you give, the more that you receive.

62-8: Obama needs an ombudsman more than anything else.

62-9: Look at the World with an open mind but, keep a guarded tongue.

62-10: You can't fix what is unfixable. But, you can, at least, try.

62-11: Everybody everywhere needs somebody sometimes but, everyone at anyplace wants something else all of the time.

62-12: Run your life like a five-star hotel but, always leave room for an honored guest.

62-13: For a wider horizon, always be nice.

62-14: Old people can act young and young people can act old but, the trick is to always be young at heart.

62-15: My father always said, "I'm nineteen inside but, outside, I am not.

62-16: The best friend that I ever had was a retired Army hero who could not learn how to stop being a soldier.

62-17: If I were single, my pockets would jingle and I would be happy again. But, I would rather be old and gray if my deceased wife could somehow stay.

62-18: They say that dead people communicate through the electric lights. And, my Dorothy turns them on about twice a month. I just say hello and bid her goodnight because I don't know how to talk to photons.

62-19: As a father, I loved my one son and I pray that he will become a better son.

62-20: Time may fly swiftly by but, I could never find a daughter as sweet as mine.

62-21: My children tell everyone how great I am. I just wish that they would say the same things to me.

62-22: Sometimes, there is more safety in pounds, not numbers. My boyhood chum was the biggest guy around and no one messed with us.

62-23: A high school buddy claimed that our graduating class was the most successful to ever graduate from Hazard High School. We were not brilliant. We were just lucky.

62-24: There is nothing wrong with having a bully on your side.

62-25: If baseball is more intellectual than football, why do baseball players scratch their crotch and chew tobacco?

62-26: Getting older is called slowing down and, in my golden years, I have been most successful so why should I slow down? I embrace old age.

62-27: The most fortunate man has two mothers, his own and the mother of his children.

62-28: My engineering life has been dedicated to solving problems and helping other people. In my mind, there is no greater goal.

62-29: Engineers give whatever they can for the benefit of mankind.

62-30: Men are baffled by a new birth.

62-31: Women are most beautiful when they are pregnant. Their face has such a warm and healthy glow.

62-32: Newborns are ugly until they are held.

62-33: Keep CHRIST in Christmas. Stop using XMAS.

62-34: Each morning should be treated as a celebrated gift.

62-35: Happiness exists when others are considered before you are.

62-36: Married young is married longer, if it is done correctly.

62-37: For the minority, married longer is the best answer for the divorce rate of today.

62-38: A well married man married well.

62-39: A divorced man will be all by his lonesome someday.

62-40: What kind of a woman would want to be an old maid? Hopefully, there is none.

62-41: Before a man should marry, he needs to be at least 25-years old.

62-42: Why are so many preachers without wives? Perhaps, they spend too much time in front of the looking glass and practicing their sermon.

62-43: Live life as I lived mine. Mecum Dictum, Mecum Pactim or (My word is my bond).

62-44: Shout before you shoot and make sure that the home invader is facing you, not running away from you. That's the difference between murder and self-defense.

62-45: Never make friends with known enemies.

62-46: Never let an enemy inside of your house.

62-47: Above all, be above most.

62-48: No one plans to fail. They just fail to plan.

62-49: Never be one nap short for each full day.

62-50: Measure once and cut twice. Measure twice and cut once.

A son who works in summer is prudent. A son who sleeps through the harvest brings shame to the family.

CHAPTER SIXTY-THREE
ITEMS 1-50

63-1: Do small things big and do big things small.

63-2: Brevity is the soul of wit.

63-3: On all matters we are each somewhat ignorant.

63-4: Disagree without being rude.

63-5: Life on Earth involves the three 'L's of learning, loving and living.

63-6: A boss is a person who is always late when you come in early but, always early when you come in late.

63-7: Never beat a dead horse.

63-8: It is better to be imitated than to be ignored.

63-9: Accordance and discordance are but a dance apart.

63-10: A father is too often measured by the load that he can haul.

63-11: There is something missing if the sum of the parts does not equal the whole.

63-12: The shorter live longer than the longer.

63-13: The larger eat more than the smaller.

63-14: The larger sees more than the shorter.

63-15: Those that love too much hurt too easily.

63-16: Be a clinging vine or the stoutest tree.

63-17: People like to add more than they care to subtract.

63-18: Incompleteness defines some completeness.

63-19: The beginning and the end can describe a life.

63-20: Order or disorder can involve a person and their distribution.

63-21: People who take part usually partake.

63-22: Better set than upset.

63-23: The wrong version is inversion.

63-24: There are but three choices in life, to lead, to follow and to observe.

63-25: The customer may not always be right but, the customer is never wrong.

63-26: Listen to learn but, write for wisdom.

63-27: It isn't over 'til it's over and don't start 'til it begins.

63-28: Be inclusive before being conclusive.

63-29: Your crowning achievement is that you survived your birthing.

63-30: Your ultimate achievement is your death.

63-31: Continuity is discontinuity united.

63-32: One can never bring his thoughts together without being focused.

63-33: Before conformity can ever be written, unconformity must first become unwritten.

63-34: When a minority speaks for the majority, that Nation is in crisis.

63-35: Welfare and faring well should not be identical.

63-36: Today should be treated as 'day two' so that we can fix things which need fixing.

63-37: Regarding orders, ask once to know and twice to be certain.

63-38: If it is said, "Therein hangs a tale", stop what you are doing and listen.

63-39: What wife would want to serve 'pickled pig's feet'?

63-40: Like father, like son, like one, or like no one.

63-41: If the shoe fits, wear it. If the shoe no longer fits, share it.

63-42: It amounts to the same thing if we want it to be.

63-43: His kind will never go this way again unless we follow his teachings.

63-44: The cart before the horse makes the statement that something is 'bass-ackwards'.

63-45: Fortunately chaos does not often exist. That is usually reserved for the Courthouse.

63-46: Blessedly, most pains are strictly temporary.

63-47: A good plot is like gravy. Both must thicken if they are to be best enjoyed.

63-48: If one falls, it is only human. If one falls into his own place, it is sublime.

63-49: If a writer is unknown, unread and unseen, that person is probably without a literary agent.

63-50: If one is legionary, he might become legendary.

A man of humble standing who works for himself is one to be reckoned with.

CHAPTER SIXTY-FOUR
ITEMS 1-50

64-1: In the name of decency, be decent. In the name of honesty, be honest. In the name of thyself, be truthful.

64-2: Thoughtful and thoughtless are widely different motivators.

64-3: If it needs to be there tomorrow, then, it needs to be gone today.

64-4: No sooner said than done but, no sooner done than argued.

64-5: It is sometimes better to touch and go than to stay without touching.

64-6: Too much spicy food will bring a doctor before dessert is served.

64-7: For an idea whose time has come, its hour will soon pass.

64-8: Never say 'that is why' without explaining 'why that is'.

64-9: Our withers are rung or not, depending on the twist.

64-10: From my railroad days, steam will rise if the shovel is full.

64-11: Birds will always leave their nest. Some will fly while others won't.

64-12: The human menagerie does exist but only in urban areas.

64-13: A breath of fresh air is when re-vitalization begins.

64-14: Not as you were or as you are but, as you ought to be.

64-15: If the bubble bursts, blame the bubble-err.

64-16: If you live on bottomland, know that outside water will soon be inside water.

64-17: A life that 'hangs by a thread' needs more reinforcement.

64-18: A race that can be won must be done.

64-19: Look beyond things, not at things.

64-20: She was as sweet as honey but, sometimes, as sour as vinegar.

64-21: Light as a feather refers to birds only.

64-22: If you want to hear a pin drop, visit a bowling alley.

64-23: Air never rings of anything but many things ring true because air is there.

64-24: As black as the tinker's pot.

64-25: As black as the ace of spades.

64-26: As blind as a bat.

64-27: Scales in the eyes must be gone if we are to see.

64-28: If you must know, weight scales seldom lie.

64-29: If you must know, it is time to go.

64-30: A mind that won't bend will seldom win.

64-31: A hand that can't catch will seldom fetch.

64-32: If it had been a snake, it would have bitten you.

64-33: Wisdom returns when concentration resumes.

64-34: If your thoughts are in the outfield, the infield suffers.

64-35: Notice given is advice taken.

64-36: All grapes are not sour.

64-37: Point given is a point that's taken.

64-38: Where Christmas is concerned, remember the reason for the season.

64-39: This yuletide, wrap less and talk more.

64-40: A neighborhood of transients isn't so bad. Nobody ever dies, they just move away.

64-41: A blind bargain is rarely the best bargain.

64-42: If doubt holds no bounds, how can there be a judgment that is beyond the shadow of a doubt?

64-43: The tax man encourages us to be successful so that he can have his share.

64-44: If Heaven knows all, what can a mere Earthling communicate?

64-45: When experts disagree, individuals must decide.

64-46: When there is nothing more that should be said, listen to your soul.

64-47: Naught ought to sell for naught.

64-48: Pleas that go to ground won't hold water.

64-49: Leather is well liked by the motorcycle guys but, cattle despise the sight of it.

64-50: Fur coats are least appreciated by their original owners.

A man of quick temper acts foolishly but a man of discretion is far more patient.

CHAPTER SIXTY-FIVE
ITEMS 1-50

65-1: Eat the hen but, always save the rooster.

65-2: Let some believe what they may but, let those who understand be in control.

65-3: A man who wants children usually desires immortality.

65-4: There is no love without pain as there is no pain without love.

65-5: Go with the wind not against the wind.

65-6: If a man can steer his mind, wisdom should be his first port-of-call.

65-7: Don't be disappointed by the things that you didn't do when there is still time to do them.

65-8: Be proud of the things that you did do but, be ashamed of what you could have done.

65-9: Wasted time is the mirror of our mind and time matters most.

65-10: Friendship nurtures survival.

65-11: Perseverance fights vacillation best.

65-12: Criticism creates an interest in things that need to be changed.

65-13: We become wiser when we are mindful of our worst mistakes.

65-14: Too many people of the same mind can be dangerous.

65-15: People with different opinions represent a challenge.

65-16: An issue that opens a person's eyes suggests that those eyes were, previously, closed.

65-17: Too much education is bad but, too little is inexcusable.

65-18: A little learning will go a long way but never far enough.

65-19: Most of the trouble in this World is caused by those who understand too little.

65-20: Washington DC had a message for us mountain people. They said, "Go tell it on the mountain."

65-21: Telling something on the mountain was our first means of communication and, all too often, our last resort.

65-22: An unbalanced mind knows a little balance.

65-23: They that move away to live with the flat-landers might read but, those that stay behind must read.

65-24: Never let a small child get away with this: "A little bird told me."

65-25: Saying "Nobody the wiser" shelters bad deeds.

65-26: When words depart, try 'lips together'.

65-27: The greatest mistake that we make needs to be our final one.

65-28: Life is more fun when we have a positive attitude and reach out to others.

65-29: People listen least to the tongue that wags the most.

65-30: The Brits made this saying famous: "At the end of the day."

65-31: Ale does more for the body than politicians can.

65-32: Those who walk in the shade never carry an umbrella.

65-33: I won't argue with you, not when I am trying to straighten you out.

65-34: What I aspired to be, comforts me because all I ever wanted to be was a published writer.

65-35: What is lovely now will always be lovely as long as she has enough make-up.

65-36: My dream of a perfect novel was lost to me after I woke up.

65-37: An ode to Congress: "If the blind do lead the blind, we all shall end up in a ditch."

65-38: A sad indication of the time in which we live is "Too many books and too few readers.

65-39: Some people have learned nothing and forgotten more.

65-40: Brevity is the backbone of wit.

65-41: Big business ought to give customers a break.

65-42: When you can't steal, cheat.

65-43: It is better to be all alone than to be in the presence of thieves.

65-44: When we have only what we dislike, we must like what we have.

65-45: God gives us meat but, the devil sends us cooks.

65-46: God may have made the Countries but, Satan sure made the Cities.

65-47: There is no place in Heaven for a professional quitter.

65-48: Culture teaches us to know the best and the worst of all acts and actors.

65-49: Self-satisfaction should be the goal of every person on Earth.

65-50: I would rather be myself than anyone else.

Actions sometimes speaks louder than words.

CHAPTER SIXTY-SIX
ITEMS 1-50

66-1: Life isn't always fair but it sure does beat the alternative.

66-2: If your future is in doubt, take the next positive step.

66-3: Hatred takes a lot of time and energy and life is too short to waste any part of it in that manner.

66-4: Your position at work won't take care of you when you are ill.

66-5: Look to your parents and your friends when you need them the most.

66-6: Stay in touch with your loved ones, they are the ones that need to hear from you on a regular basis.

66-7: Don't spend more than you make.

66-8: Each month, you should try to pay more than the minimum on your credit card accounts.

66-9: You don't have to win every argument, try to compromise.

66-10: Don't cry alone. It helps to have someone else to cry with.

66-11: God, the one who created the Universe, is a tough person. So, it is okay to get angry with him. He can take it and he wants to help, angry or not.

66-12: Put some of your first paycheck away for retirement. You will need it more at that time.

66-13: Chocolate is irresistible. It's best if you learn how to ration your intake.

66-14: Everyone has a past, make peace with yours.

66-15: An unrepaired past can mess up the future.

66-16: You don't have to hide when you cry. We all know how to cry.

66-17: If your children have seen you cry, that's all right because you have seen them cry, many times over.

66-18: Don't compare your life to others. Each of us is different.

66-19: Everyone's journey on Earth assumes a different path.

66-20: If a relationship must be kept secret, you shouldn't be involved.

66-21: Everything can change in the blink of an eye. But, don't worry, God can keep track of all things at any speed.

66-22: Take a deep breath and count to ten before you hurt someone's feelings.

66-23: Get rid of anything that bothers you, isn't useful or frightens you.

66-24: Keep all things that you like, no matters what others might say.

66-25: Whatever doesn't permanently maim you makes you stronger.

66-26: Having a second childhood could prove harmful, be careful.

66-27: If writing is what you like to do best, then write.

66-28: Burn the candles or light the midnight oil but, always do your best.

66-29: A woman that won't use the expensive perfume and refuses to wear her most provocative undies or saves the Egyptian Cotton sheets for another day might be more lonesome than she wants to be.

66-30: Be like the Scouts, be always prepared and, then, go to wherever it takes you.

66-31: Be as eccentric as you can because eccentric people get noticed.

66-32: No other person is in charge of your unhappiness except you. And, no other person can do something about it except you.

66-33: When you have a personal crisis, ask yourself if you will remember it 5-years from now or 10-years from now? That's a good way to classify the seriousness of your personal problems.

66-34: Always choose life over suicide. The latter is illegal in God's eyes.

66-35: Forgive everyone everything and your slate will be clean.

66-36: What others say about you is none of your business.

66-37: The passing of time heals everything if you just let time pass.

66-38: However awful, anything that seems real bad must be changed.

66-39: Don't take yourself so seriously, No other person does.

66-40: Believe in miracles. They do exist and I have seen several in my lifetime.

66-41: Don't measure life. Show up and be counted.

66-42: Life doesn't come wrapped-up like a Christmas present but it is still a gift.

66-43: All that really matters at the end of the day is that you were truly loved.

66-44: Your great-grand-children have only one childhood.

66-45: Life is like a traffic jam. When you need to yield, please yield.

66-46: God loves each of us, no matter what we did or didn't do.

66-47: The poet Browning said, "The best part of life is the final part." Never argue with Mr. Browning. He's smarter than most of us.

66-48: Jealousy and greed are the worst attributes that anyone could possess.

66-49: When I was young, I fell out of trees, received several lacerations, broke my nose, cracked some other bones and lost a few teeth. But, not one lawyer filed a lawsuit about these injuries. Those were the good old days.

66-50: No healthy person wants to die.

AUTHOR PROFILE

Charles Hays was brought into this World as the son of Sally Ann Hays (Hounshell) and Courtney Cash Hays. He was a railroader and she was a stay-at-home school teacher. Whatever I am I owe so much to them, especially with respect to my Mother. She taught me what the City School teachers overlooked and her homework was much tougher than that which the City teachers gave to the other students. She wanted me to excel and I did the best that I could for her. For example, I had to read ten pages of the dictionary every day when I was a very young child and just learning how to read.

When I was about ten years old, she bought me a 1929 Portable Typewriter which I still possess. I used that machine to obtain a job with the Hazard Daily Herald where I became a Cub Reporter. I covered high school events, sports and the local Courthouse events, even the murder trials. I found them to be very interesting. Remember that, in those days, we had nothing but the radio. As a result, our newspaper was very well read and just about everyone in town was a subscriber. I wrote for the Herald until I was about nineteen. Then, the Korean Conflict arrived which forced me to leave my valley so green.

What followed was the University with three engineering degrees, a beautiful wife and two wonderful children, Brenda and Charles. Then, my resume included travel, fame and fortune as a day job. But, my hobby was still that of a storyteller. I wrote for fun and placed all my articles on the book shelves to collect dust balls. Since that time, I have published nine different books, including the current book, 'Appalachian Sayings'. In 1916, Mom started collecting old sayings as her hobby and she encouraged me to do likewise. Please enjoy our joint collection.